CRIMINAL JUSTICE

THIRD EDITION

From the Constitutional Rights Foundation and Scholastic

LIVING LAW
CRIMINAL JUSTICE

THIRD EDITION

SCHOLASTIC INC.

The preparation of these materials was financially assisted through a federal grant from the Law Enforcement Assistance Administration of the U.S. Justice Department and the California Office of Criminal Justice Planning and under Title 1 of the Crime Control Act of 1973.

Titles in the Living Law Program

Criminal Justice
Civil Justice

Staff for the Living Law Program

For the Constitutional Rights Foundation

Principal Writers and Editors
Carl Martz
Rebecca Novelli

Contributors
Mary Furlong
Nancy Boyarsky
Eric Jacobson
Louise Weinberg Jacobson

Supervisory Editors
Todd Clark
Richard Weintraub

Constitutional Rights Foundation Staff
Vivian Monroe, Executive Director
Todd Clark, Education Director
Kathleen Stewart, Associate Education Director
Carolyn Pereira, Executive Director, Chicago/National Project
Marshall Croddy, Director of Publications

Constitutional Rights Foundation Board of Directors
Judge William P. Hogoboom, President
Stuart D. Buchalter, Vice President
Raymond C. Fisher, Vice President
Justice Arleigh M. Woods, Vice President
Marvin Sears, Secretary
Lloyd M. Smith, Treasurer

Publications Committee
Jerome C. Byrne, Chairman
Bayard Berman
Julia Rider
Lloyd M. Smith

Law, Education And Participation (LEAP) Project
National Committee

James J. Brice, Co-Chairman, Arthur Anderson & Co., Chicago, Illinois
Willie Campbell, President, Overseas Education Fund of the League of Women Voters, Los Angeles, California
James A. Cobey, Retired Judge, California Court of Appeal, Los Angeles, California
Joseph M. Cronin, President, Massachusetts Higher Education Assistance Corporation, Boston, Massachusetts

No part of this publication may be reproduced in whole or in part, or stored in a retrieval system, or transmitted in any form or by any means, electronic, mechanical, photocopying, or otherwise, without written permission of the publisher. For information regarding permissions, write to Scholastic Inc., 730 Broadway, New York, NY 10003.
ISBN 0-590-34828-0

Copyright 1988, 1984, 1978 by Scholastic Inc. All rights reserved. Published by Scholastic Inc.
12 11 10 9 8 7 6 5 4

0/9 1
23

Printed in the U.S.A.

Margaret C. Driscoll, Chief Judge, Connecticut Juvenile Court, Past President, National Council of Juvenile Court Judges, Bridgeport, Connecticut

Robert H. Hall, Judge, U.S. District Court, Atlanta, Georgia

Patrick Head, Vice-President & General Counsel, FMC Corp., Chicago, Illinois

Pat Healy, Executive Director, Chicago Crime Commission, Chicago, Illinois

Carla A. Hills, Attorney, Latham, Watkins & Hills, Washington, D.C.

David Hornbeck, State Superintendent of Public Instruction, Baltimore, Maryland

Peter Liacouras, President, Temple University, Philadelphia, Pennsylvania

Scott Matheson, Governor, Utah, Salt Lake City, Utah

Richard Maxwell, Professor, Duke University School of Law, Durham, North Carolina

Floretta McKenzie, Superintendent of Schools, Washington, D.C.

E. Leo Milonas, Justice, Appellate Division, First Department, New York, New York

Dorothy Nelson, Judge, U.S. Court of Appeals, 9th Circuit, Los Angeles, California

Ewald B. Nyquist, Vice-President, Pace University, Former Commissioner of Education, New York, Petersburg, New York

Craig Phillips, State Superintendent of Public Instruction, Raleigh, North Carolina

John Porter, President, Eastern Michigan University, Ypsilanti, Michigan

Cruz Reynoso, Justice, California Supreme Court, San Francisco, California

Ann Riley, Governor's Task Force on Citizen Participation and Education, Columbus, South Carolina

K. Eugene Shutler, Attorney, Troy, Malin, Pottinger & Casden, Los Angeles, California

Isidore Starr, Professor Emeritus, Queens College, Scottsdale, Arizona

J. Graham Sullivan, Retired Deputy Superintendent, Los Angeles Unified Schools, Danville, California

Dan Walker, Former Governor, Illinois, Chicago, Illinois

Pearl West, Past Director, California Youth Authority, Stockton, California

Constitutional Rights Foundation wishes to thank the following attorneys and legal professionals who reviewed the content of this publication:

William W. Bedsworth, Deputy District Attorney, Orange County; Mark A. Borenstein, Tuttle & Taylor; Anita Susan Brenner, Deputy Public Defender, Los Angeles County; Alvin B. Calof, Court Commissioner, Los Angeles Superior Court; Nancy Sher Cohen, Tuttle & Taylor; Douglas C. Conroy, Paul, Hastings, Janofsky & Walker; James B. Ekins, Southern California Counsel, Mobil Land Development Corporation; Howard W. Gillingham, Attorney; David M. Houston-Reeve, Gibson, Dunn & Crutcher; Jeffrey A. Maldonado, Tuttle & Taylor; Franz E. Miller, Deputy District Attorney, Orange County; James Odlum, Gibson, Dunn, & Crutcher; Susan B. Oman, Mitchell, Silverberg & Knupp; Julia J. Rider, Luce, Forward, Hill, Jeffer, & Mangels; Dick Simonian, Superintendent, C.K. Wakefield School (Fresno County Probation Dept.); Joshua Stein, Irell & Manella; Robert S. Stern, Tuttle & Taylor; Richard W. Tillson, Chief of Support Services, Department of Youth Authority; Daniel H. Willick, McKenna, Conner & Cuneo.

For Scholastic (Third Edition)
Publisher: Eleanor Angeles
Project Editors: William Johnson, Elise Bauman
Editorial Director: Carolyn Jackson
Art Director: Marijka Kostiw
Cover: James Sarfati
Illustrators: Ivan Powell, Bob Barner, Christopher Zacharow, Yvette S. Benek

Contents

Introduction: The System and You 6

Part 1: Crime and the System 10
　Chapter 1: Getting to the Memphis Five 11
　Chapter 2: Crime, Criminals, and Victims 35
　Chapter 3: The Law 47
　Chapter 4: Criminal Law and the Bill of Rights 52
　Bibliography 59

Part 2: The Badge 60
　Chapter 5: The Badge 61
　Chapter 6: The Police and Privacy 70
　Chapter 7: Arrest and Your Rights 82
　Chapter 8: Police Power 96
　Bibliography 109

Part 3: The Gavel 110
　Chapter 9: The Right to a Fair Trial 111
　Chapter 10: Lawyers and Law 120
　Chapter 11: The Trial 128
　Chapter 12: Juvenile Justice 148
　Bibliography 159

Part 4: The Bars *160*
  Chapter 13: The Problem of Punishment 161
  Chapter 14: Behind Bars 174
  Chapter 15: Probation 179
  Chapter 16: Parole 185
  Chapter 17: Youth Behind Bars 194
  Chapter 18: The Death Penalty 201
  Bibliography 209

Conclusion: What Are the Choices? 210

Chartreads
  Crime Wave 39
  Opinion Poll 45
  Recidivism 166

Glossary *214*
Index *219*

INTRODUCTION

The System and You

How does the criminal justice system work? And how does that system relate to you?

You probably think you can answer these questions without too much trouble. The world of crime and criminal justice is one of violence and strife. It is peopled by hardened criminals, tough cops, smart lawyers, and wise judges. It's easy to get this view from watching the way television and movies portray the system.

If this is your view, you probably feel that the world of criminal justice has no relation to your life. After all, you may have no plans to be a tough cop, smart lawyer, wise judge, or hardened criminal.

But TV and movies aim to entertain us. And to do this, they must often distort what really happens. They must tie their stories into neat little hour-long packages. They must show people as stereotypes. And they must emphasize action and violence.

This book has two main purposes. One is to show you how

the system really works. The other is to show you how that system fits into your life.

You may be surprised at the many ways the system touches the average law-abiding citizen. Some citizens may be called for jury duty. That is one important way in which the system may affect you. Other ways arise out of crime and the fear of crime. Some of you will become direct victims of crime. All of you will have your lives affected in some way by crime.

You may not stay out late at night for fear of crime in the streets. You may stop going to places you once enjoyed. You will pay higher prices for products because of shoplifting. You will pay higher taxes to raise the public funds used to fight crime. As this book makes clear, we are *all* victims of crime.

The system may also affect you in your choice of career. Law and police work are the best known of the many careers in the criminal justice system. But this book also explores other career possibilities.

Finally, the book treats our rights as American citizens. It relates how these rights must be balanced against the need of our society to protect itself against crime. You will see how our courts are constantly trying to balance these opposing forces.

This book has four parts. The first, called "The System," gives an overview. The second, "The Badge," deals with police work. "The Gavel" examines our court system. "The Bars" studies our corrections system. Each of these parts is designed to teach you, interest you, and most of all, to challenge you. There are stories, role-playing exercises, interviews, suggestions for inviting resource people into the classroom, suggestions for outside activities, and skills exercises.

When you finish this book, you will know how the system works. You'll also have a clear picture of the many ways the criminal justice system relates to your life.

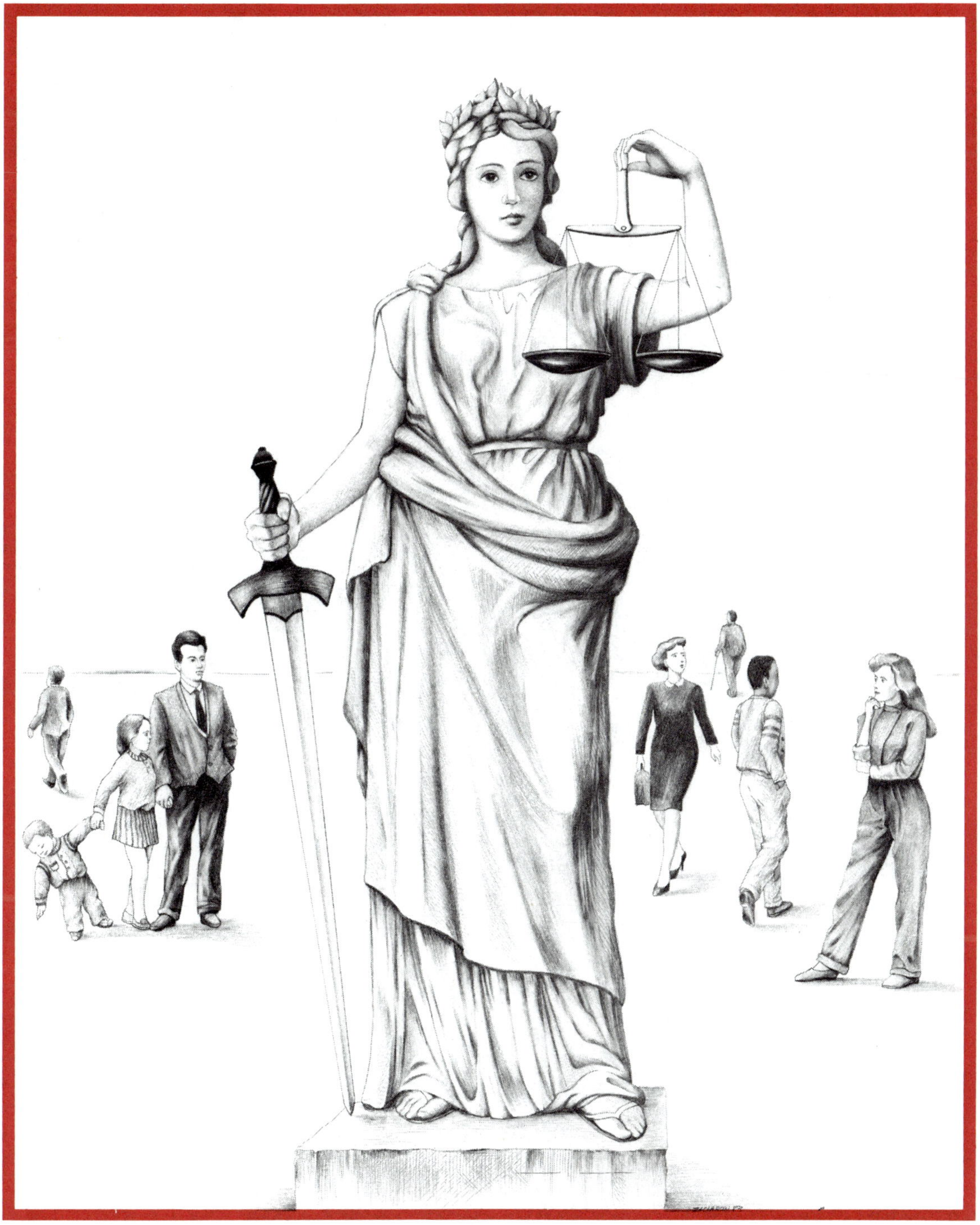

PART 1
CRIME
and the SYSTEM

Chapter 1
Getting to the Memphis Five

This chapter introduces the real system of criminal justice. It points up some differences between adult and juvenile justice. It focuses on the key people who make the system work. It shows how each part of the system comes together in the case of John Singleton and Laurie Dorman. These parts are the law, constitutional rights, police work, courts, and corrections.

Most of all, this chapter is about people. John, 18, and Laurie, 17, are arrested for car theft. The difference in their ages is crucial.

John must go through the adult criminal justice system. Laurie goes through the juvenile justice system. (For more on juvenile justice, see pages 148-158.) This experience brings John and Laurie in touch with lawyers, public defenders, police officers, witnesses, district attorneys, judges, and probation officers. They must deal with bail, plea bargaining, and sentencing. Through their story, you will have a chance to test your values and opinions on some of the main issues in criminal justice today.

174

The crime

Laurie Dorman came to the door holding a copy of *Rolling Stone* in her hands. Her long, dark hair fell to her shoulders and over her white dress.

"Hi, John. What are you doing here?"

She's really pretty, John thought. He hesitated. "Uh . . . well, my mom's mad at me again because I'm not working, and she's yellin' at me, so I just went for a walk and, uh, here I am."

"Gee, that's too bad," Laurie mumbled. She was thinking of something else.

"Are you going to ask me in?" John asked.

"I can't, John. You know my father doesn't want you in the house when no one is around. He doesn't think you're reliable. You know, not having a job." Laurie's voice trailed off, embarrassed.

John winced. He remembered how he had argued with his own mother over the same issue. He tried again. "You just don't want to let me in, Laurie," he went on.

"No, I can't. My parents said no."

"Come on, just for a little while," John coaxed.

"What if old Gregory, across the street, saw us? I'll bet he's looking out the window at us right now. If we got caught, you'd give it all away because you're a bad liar."

"Maybe you could teach me," John shot back.

Laurie pouted. "Just for that, you can take me to see the Memphis Five at the Auditorium tonight. It's a special deal — three dollars with this coupon." She pointed to an ad in *Rolling Stone*. "You can do that, can't you?" Laurie prodded.

"It's not the money, Laurie. I just can't get a car. My dad's mad at me and so is my mom. How about your —"

"They're going out of town," she cut in. "Look, John, I won't take three buses to get there. If you can't get a car, I'll go with Tony. He called this afternoon."

"I don't know what else I can do, Laurie." John waited. "I'll try," he said finally. "I'll see you later." As he went down the front walk, he noticed Mr. Gregory standing in his doorway across the street. John felt in his pockets. Seven dollars and some change. He walked several blocks to a phone booth and called Mike.

"Sorry, man, but I got three couples in my car already," said Mike. "Did you call Andy?"

"No. His car's all torn down," John said.

John hung up. No car, no girl, he thought. But Laurie might still change her mind. It's worth a try, John decided.

The choice

She was standing on the porch that evening as he came up the walk.

"Did you get a car?" Laurie asked.

"No. I tried, but —"

"Listen, I've got an idea," Laurie said. "I know where you can get a car."

"Where?"

"Next door."

"Whose is it?"

"Our neighbors'."

"They said we could borrow it?" John asked uneasily.

"No. The Porters are away on vacation."

"Laurie, that isn't even borrowing. It's stealing."

"The keys are on the seat. They won't know. They won't be back till next week. Nobody will know. We'll bring it back after the concert."

"I can't, Laurie."

"I want to see the Memphis Five, John." She paused. "I told Tony I'd call him by seven if I didn't have a date."

John took a deep breath. "Oh, all right. But we're going to get back early, just to be safe. We'll come right home. If anything happens, we got the keys from the, uh. . . ."

"Porters. Wilbert Porter."

John was nervous as he backed the car out of the driveway and drove toward the city. Neither he nor Laurie saw Mr. Gregory come out his front door as they rode down the street.

Parking was expensive near the Auditorium. John decided to park

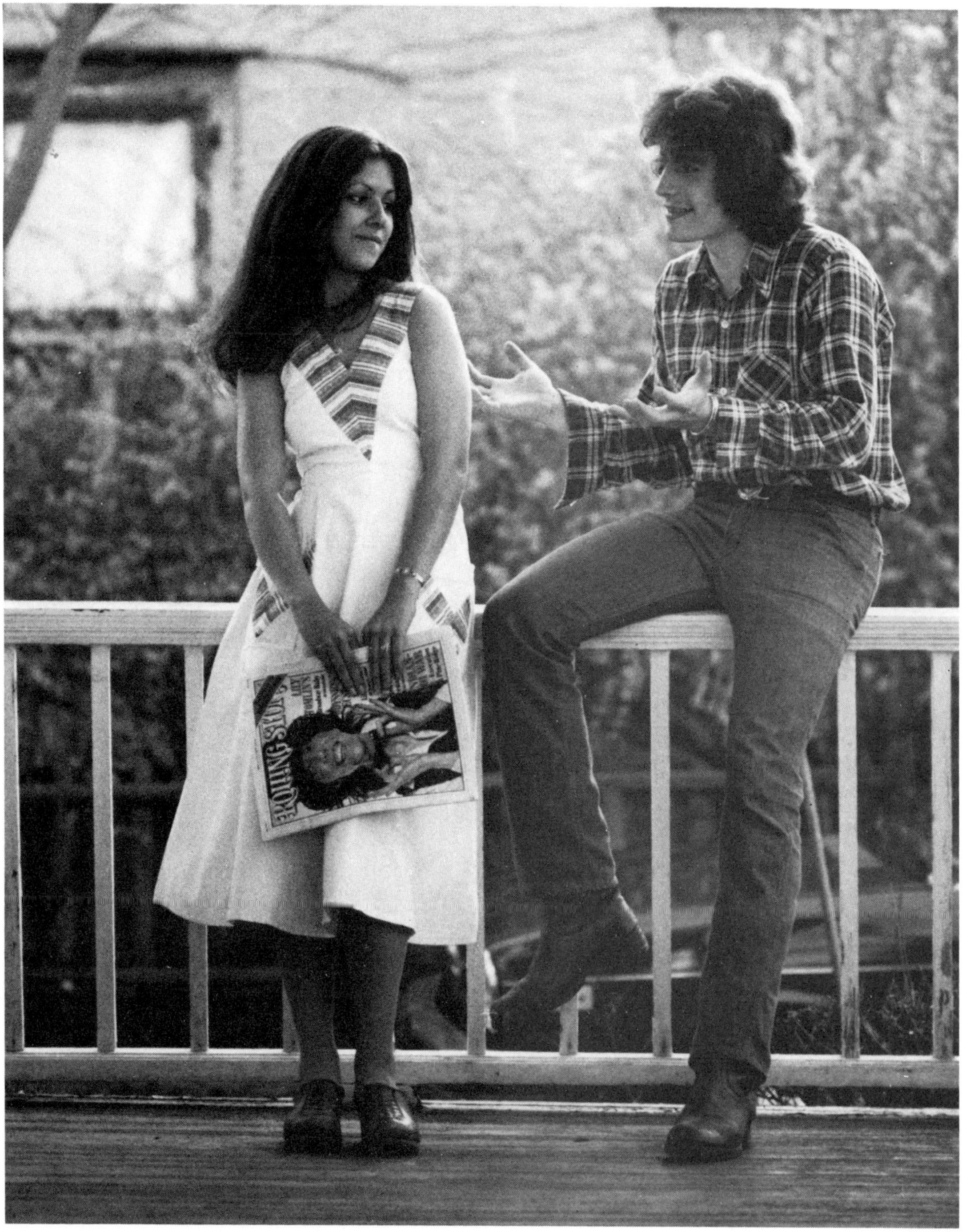

on the street. In their hurry to get to the concert, neither John nor Laurie saw that they had parked in a no-parking zone. When they finally reached the Auditorium, it was crowded, and they had to sit in the back. But they forgot themselves as the Memphis Five began their first song.

Your Turn

1. What were the main steps which led John and Laurie to take the Porters' car? At what point did John or Laurie (or both) first break the law?

2. What kind of person is John? What kind of person is Laurie? How do you think their personalities affected what happened?

3. Did either John or Laurie think it was wrong to take the car? Who do you think was more responsible for taking it? Why?

4. What would you have done if you had been John? What would you have done if you had been Laurie?

The stakeout

A patrol car pulled up to a hot-dog stand near the Auditorium. One of the officers in the car was talking on the radio: "This is Davis, car 40. Checking out a 1977 Ford Galaxie, blue, two-door sedan. AGM, Adam, George, Mary. Three, four, seven."

"Just a moment, 40," the dispatcher said. "That car was reported stolen at about seven this evening from the residence of Wilbert Porter on Stanley Drive."

The officer looked over to his partner. "Well, we've got a hot one," he said. "Probably they're over at the Auditorium."

Davis, a veteran of 15 years on the force, saw his partner, Berman, reading. Berman was a rookie. "Still studying?" Davis asked. "When I went to the Police Academy, we had stress training — I mean tough stuff. It was like boot camp. None of this sociology and psychology that you guys are studying. You'll probably end up a chief, and I'll still be up all night in this patrol car."

"Lay off, Davis," Berman protested. "I've got to read this before the crowd gets out."

"Too bad, Berman, because the show is letting out right now. We'll let them get in the car and drive away. That way we'll meet the rule that they have to drive a stolen car before it's a crime. We also won't run any chance of trouble from the crowd during the arrest."

"Good police work, there, Davis. I think we'll keep you on. Look. Here they come."

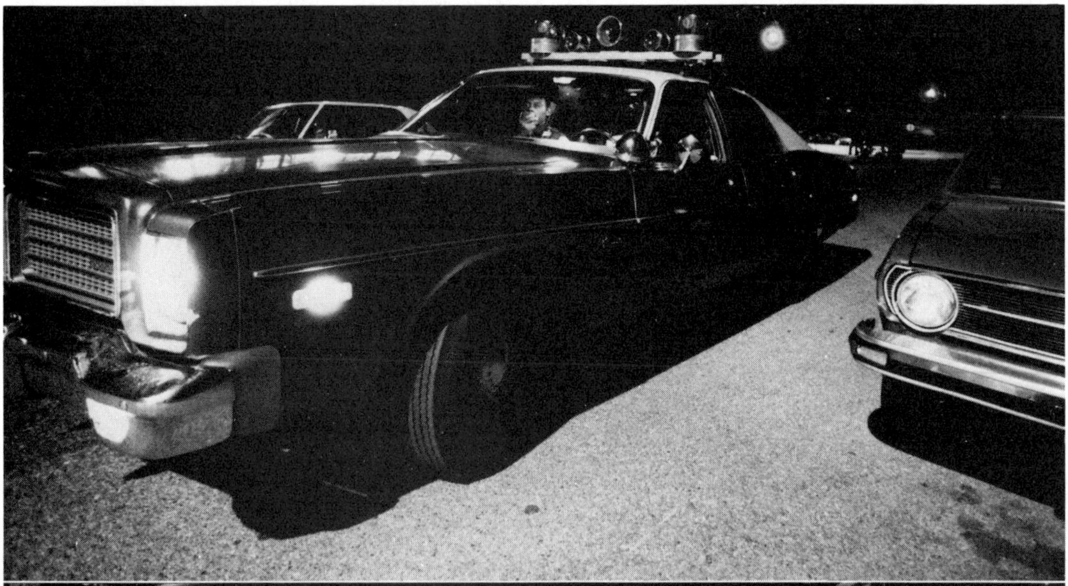

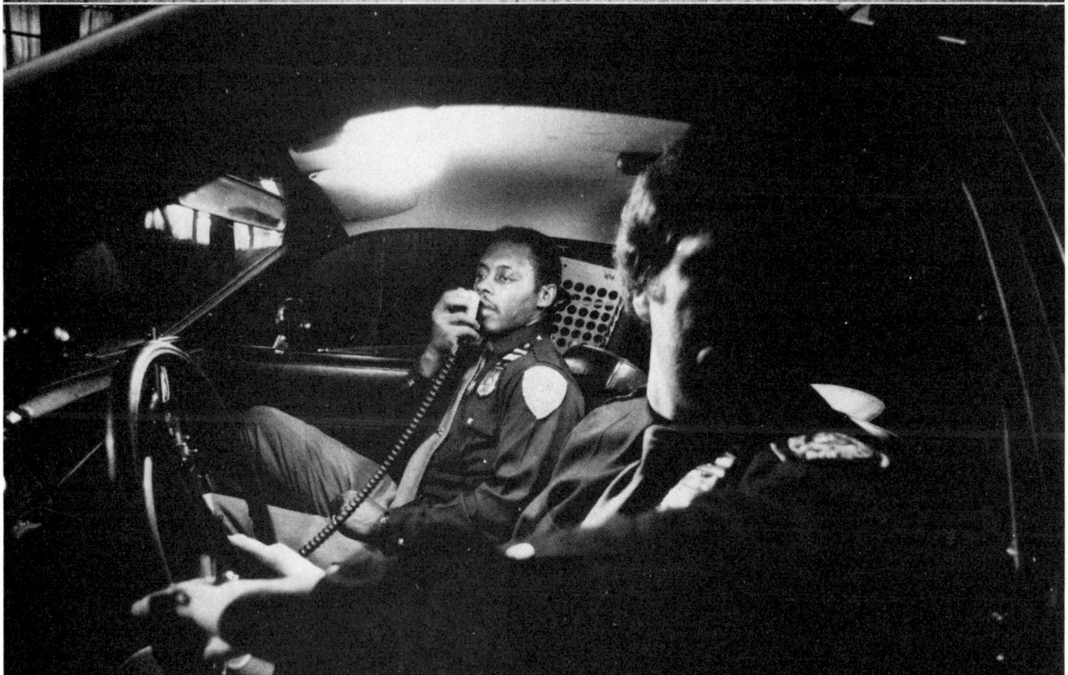

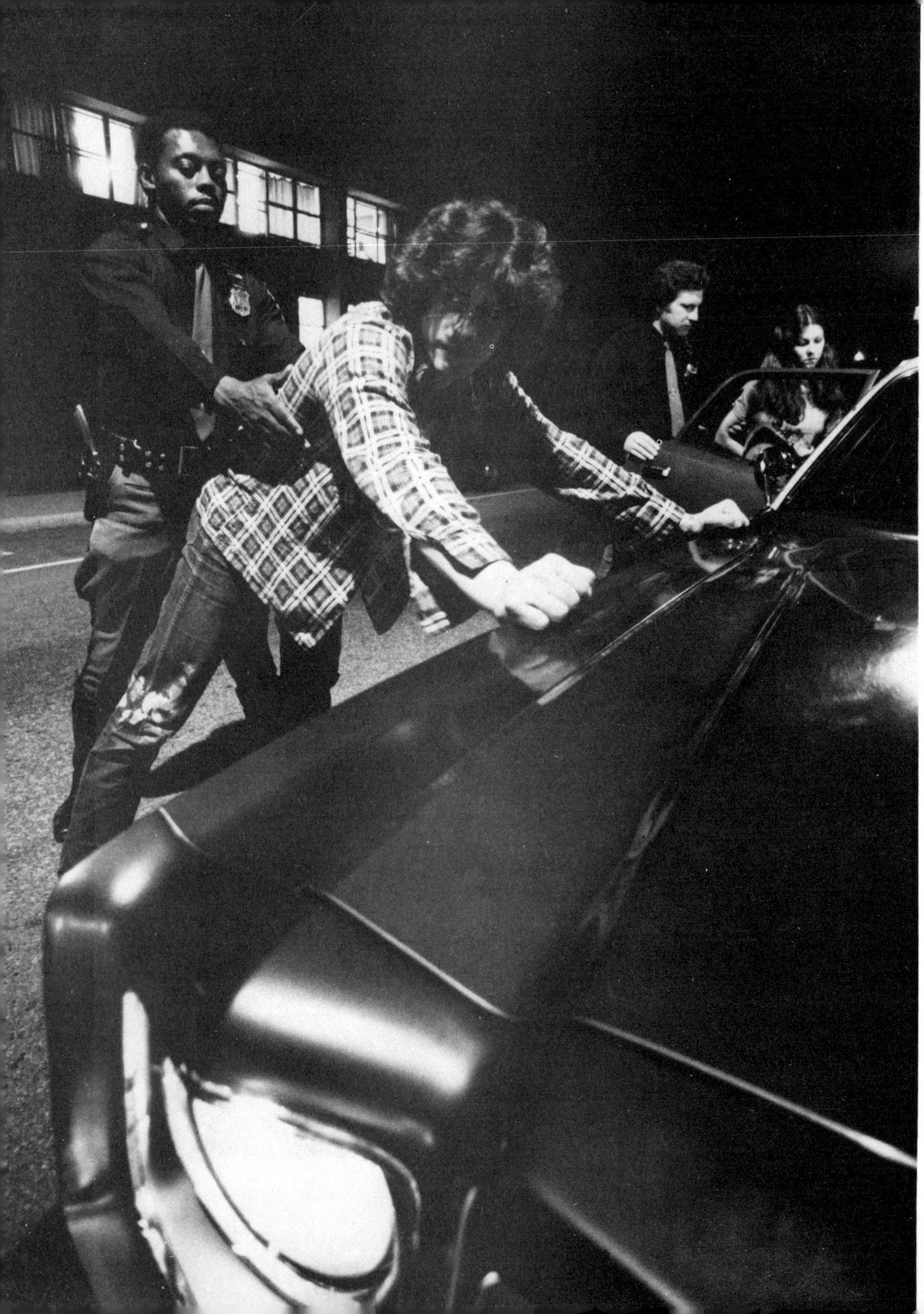

Busted

"John, I think there's a police car behind us," Laurie said weakly.

"Geez, the red light's on. I've got to pull over. Wonder what's wrong."

John pulled off to the side and stopped the car. It seemed to him that Davis was at the door instantly. "All right, kid, let me see your driver's license."

"What's wrong?" John asked as he got out. Berman was on the other side of the car shining a flashlight on Laurie.

"This car has been reported stolen. Do you have the registration?"

"I think so," John said. "It's probably in the glove compartment."

Berman stopped him. "Just a minute," he said. "Get out, put your palms on the car, and spread your feet." Berman frisked John. "All right, get the registration. And you," he said to Laurie, "come over here." Laurie stood by the officers while John fumbled around in the glove compartment. He handed the registration to Berman.

"Your name isn't Porter," the officer said.

Davis stepped in. "You have the right to remain silent. Anything you say can and will be used against you in a court of law. You have the right to speak to a lawyer and to have the lawyer present during questioning. If you so desire, and cannot afford one, a lawyer will be appointed without any charge before any questioning. Do you understand these rights as I have explained them to you?"

"Yes," John said, quietly.

Laurie nodded. "I think so."

Berman told John to put his hands behind his back. The snap of the handcuffs seemed very loud despite the traffic noise.

"Put your hands behind your back now, young lady," Berman said as he snapped on the cuffs.

Laurie and John were silent during the drive to the police station.

The booking

"This is a male-female arrest," Berman said to the sergeant. "The female is a juvenile. Grand theft, auto."

A deputy led Laurie away to be booked and searched at the juvenile division. After booking, Laurie was taken to a large room where she sat alone nervously looking at old magazines while a sergeant tried to locate her parents by telephone. After a while, the sergeant came in and

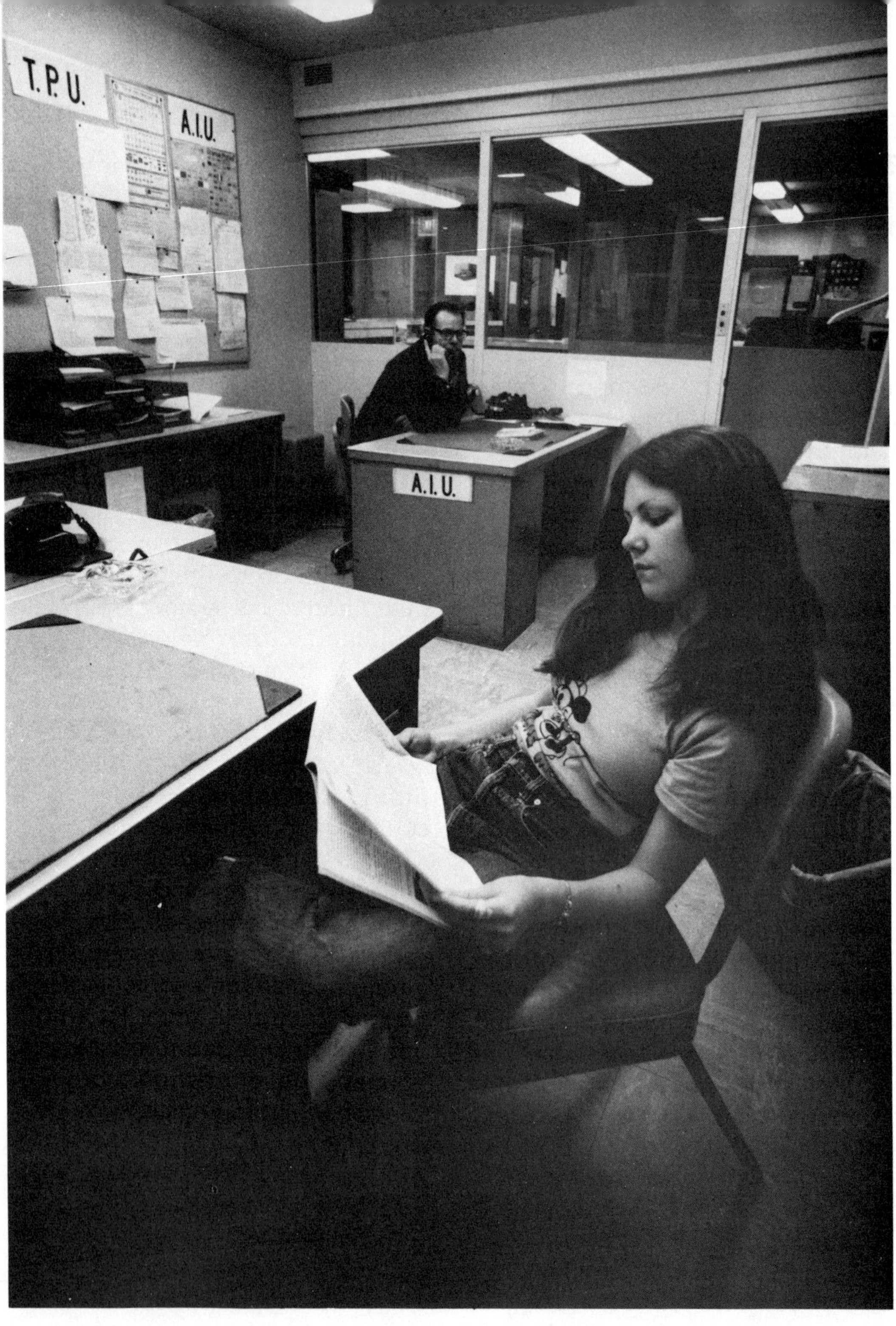
T.P.U.
A.I.U.
A.I.U.

said, "We just got your parents. They're coming right in. You can go home with them."

Meanwhile, in the adult division, John was trying to phone his parents. There was no answer.

"I want a lawyer," John said to the sergeant.

"You have the right to a lawyer while you're being questioned. But it's after midnight now and tomorrow is Saturday. We won't question you until Monday. Can you put up *bail**?"

"I don't have any money," John replied.

"Normally, we would release you on your own word," the sergeant explained. "But you have a record for joyriding and there's no one home, so we'll have to hold you." John was led to a cell. He lay awake on the hard bunk for a long time.

Your Turn

1. Why did the police officers decide not to arrest John and Laurie until after they had driven the car away?

2. Why were John and Laurie taken to different areas of the police station?

3. What kind of information did the police find about John after he was brought to the police station? How did this affect him?

4. Do you think John and Laurie have thus far been treated fairly by the justice system?

5. In your opinion, is either John or Laurie a criminal?

---

*See the Glossary at the back of this book for the meaning of any unusual words.

Before the trial

The next day, John stood before a judge who asked him if he had money for a lawyer. When John said no, the judge appointed a public defender to his case. The judge set bail at $150. John's parents put up the money, and he then went home with them.

Ten days later, John sat in a courtroom at the defense table. He was silent as Mary Burns, the public defender assigned to his case, explained what would probably happen at the hearing.

"This is a hearing, not a trial," she said. "The deputy district attorney will present his case against you. The judge will then decide if there is reason to hold you for trial."

The hearing was brief. Wilbert Porter, owner of the car, testified that he had not given anyone permission to borrow his car. Mr. Gregory, the neighbor across the street, stated that he saw a man and a woman drive away in the car belonging to Porter. Patrolman Berman identified John as the man he had arrested in the car later that evening.

After the testimony had been presented, the deputy district attorney, George Armer, asked that John be brought to trial on the charge of grand theft, auto. The judge declared that enough evidence had been brought out in the hearing to call for a trial. He then ordered John to appear in court in one week to plead guilty or not guilty.

John slumped down with his head in his hands after hearing this. Ms. Burns tried to cheer him up: "Remember, this wasn't a trial. I still think I can defend you against the charge. We're going to plead not guilty."

"OK," John said, without any confidence.

"We'll show that the Porters left their keys in the car," Burns continued, "and that Laurie told you the Porters wouldn't mind if you used their car. You *borrowed* the car and planned to return it after the concert. You made a mistake, but didn't intend to steal. Isn't that the way it happened?"

"Yes," John said.

Plea bargaining

John pleaded not guilty to the charge of grand theft, auto, the following week. The judge then set the date for his trial in 30 days. The next day, the public defender Burns, met with Armer, the deputy district attorney.

"George, in order to make this charge stick, you've got to prove that John actually planned to keep

Police Dept.
AMBULANCE NE 2-2000
FIRE NE 2-6700
POLICE NE 2-2000
APRIL-1977
AUTO THEFT!
CHILD ABUSE

the car after the concert. We can show that he intended to return it. You can easily lose your case. However, the boy might be willing to plead guilty to a lesser charge, like joyriding, if you would drop the grand theft, auto, charge."

"Joyriding is only a misdemeanor, not a felony," Armer said. "This boy already has a previous record. We can't accept a misdemeanor charge in this case. Maybe the judge would agree to a lesser felony. What about driving without the owner's permission?"

Later that afternoon, the two lawyers talked with the judge. The judge agreed to accept a guilty plea to a lesser felony. Mary Burns then went to the jail to ask John if he would agree to plead guilty under the reduced charge. (For more on plea bargaining, see page 117.)

Juvenile intake

The day following Laurie's arrest, she and her mother went to the courthouse for a meeting with a probation officer. The purpose of this meeting was for the probation officer to decide if further legal action should be taken against Laurie. It was a long wait before Laurie was called, and both she and her mother were worried.

The probation officer was patient. He told Laurie that John had been charged that morning with grand theft, auto. He said that because the offense was so serious, he had decided to take Laurie to juvenile court.

The probation officer tried to reassure Laurie's mother. "A juvenile court hearing is something like a trial, Mrs. Dorman. But it's conducted more informally. This means there will not be any reporters present and the court records will not be made public."

Mrs. Dorman nodded.

"A juvenile court decision is based on the question: 'How can we help the child?' We're not as concerned as an adult court with the question: 'Do we have a case to get a conviction?'"

Then he asked Laurie to explain what had happened the night of her arrest.

"It's simple," Laurie said. "John picked me up and we went to the concert. Afterward we were arrested because John was driving a stolen car."

"Don't you think it's odd that John could be driving a car that belonged to your neighbor without your knowing more about it?"

"Well, he did," Laurie insisted.

Your Turn

1. The discussion between John's public defender and the deputy district attorney is usually called *plea bargaining*. From what you have read, how would you define plea bargaining?
2. Do you think John should accept the plea bargain and plead guilty to "driving without the owner's consent"? Why or why not?
3. In what ways have the experiences of John and Laurie thus far been similar? Different? Why do you think these differences exist?

Laurie's day in court

Four weeks after Laurie and her mother met with the probation officer, they returned to the courthouse for Laurie's hearing. Laurie was frightened as she entered the hearing room. But as she looked around, she could see that there was no place for a jury to sit. There was no room for spectators. This made her feel a little easier. She took a deep breath.

The district attorney called Fred Gregory to the stand.

"What happened about seven on that Saturday night?"

Mr. Gregory hesitated. "Someone took the Porters' car," he said slowly. "Two people, I think. Man and a woman. It was too dark to tell for sure. But I saw the car drive away. And I knew Will and Miriam Porter were out of town."

Laurie's attorney had no questions. Officer Berman then took the stand. He explained the circumstances of the stakeout and the arrest of Laurie and John.

John was called next. He took the oath and sat down. He said that it was Laurie's suggestion to take the car. John also said that he had agreed only when she assured him it would be all right.

Laurie was next on the stand. Her voice trembled as she took the oath. She had difficulty holding her right hand still.

"I had a date with John to go to a concert," she began. "But I told him I wouldn't go unless he would drive me. John knew how much I wanted to go and I thought he had lots of friends he could borrow a car from. So I didn't think much of it when we got in the car. I feel like it's all my fault. But I didn't mean to take a car with him, honest I didn't." Laurie began to sob.

The judge recessed the court while he considered the case. Thirty minutes later the judge gave his decision. "Laurie Dorman," he began, "this court

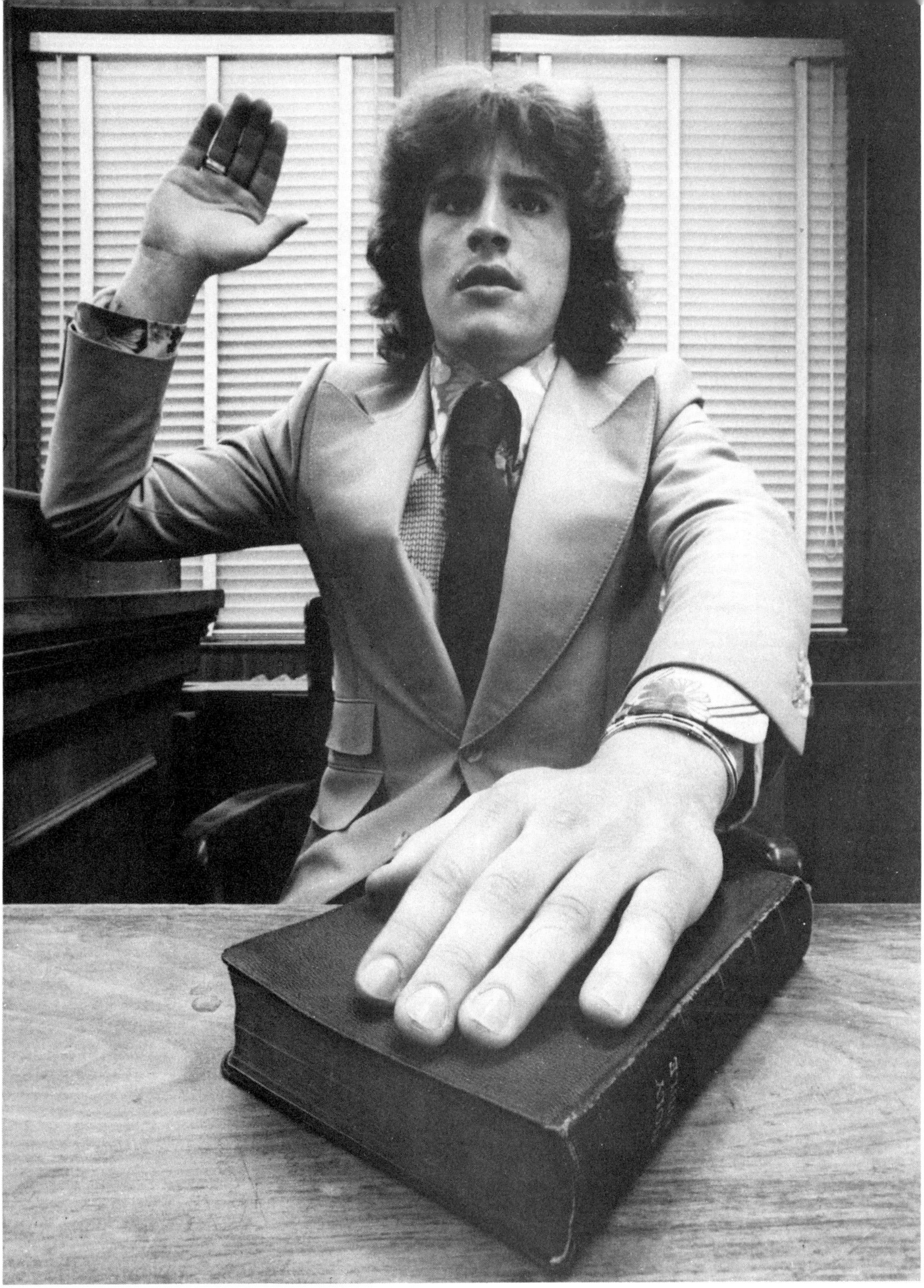

does not find you to be delinquent under the laws of this state. However, before discharging you, I would like to see you and your parents in my chambers. This hearing is finished."

Laurie breathed a sigh of relief. Then she, her parents, and her lawyer entered the judge's chambers.

"Laurie," the judge began, "I'd like to explain my ruling to you and ask your cooperation. The state could not prove, beyond a reasonable doubt, that you were guilty of any crime. But even you must admit that it seems strange that you could live next door to the family from which the car was stolen and not know more than you admit."

Laurie kept her eyes down.

"What I am asking now," the judge continued, "is that you become involved with a group activity in the community." He turned to Mr. and Mrs. Dorman. "And I am asking you to cooperate in this. Understand that the court cannot force you to do this. I just think it would be a very good first step."

The judge slid his chair back, a signal that the meeting was over. Laurie, her parents, and her lawyer stepped into the long marble corridor of the courthouse and walked to the elevators at the end of the hall. They were all silent.

John's trial

Three weeks after Laurie's case was dismissed, John went to trial.

John had decided not to accept the plea bargain Ms. Burns had proposed. Instead, he asked for a jury trial on the charge of grand theft, auto. In the courtroom, a jury was present and strangers were permitted to watch the trial. John remembered the privacy that Laurie had been allowed, and he felt jealous.

John listened as the prosecution called the witnesses. Laurie stated that John had taken her to the concert in a car like the one the Porters owned. But she claimed that she did not know where John had got the car.

During the cross-examination, Ms. Burns asked, "Laurie, didn't you suggest that John take the car just for the evening?"

"No," replied Laurie.

Mr. Gregory, Laurie's neighbor, testified he saw the car being driven down the street. Officers Berman and Davis described how they found the car and then made the arrest. Porter testified that he had not given anyone permission to use his car while he was away.

Finally, it was the defense's turn

28

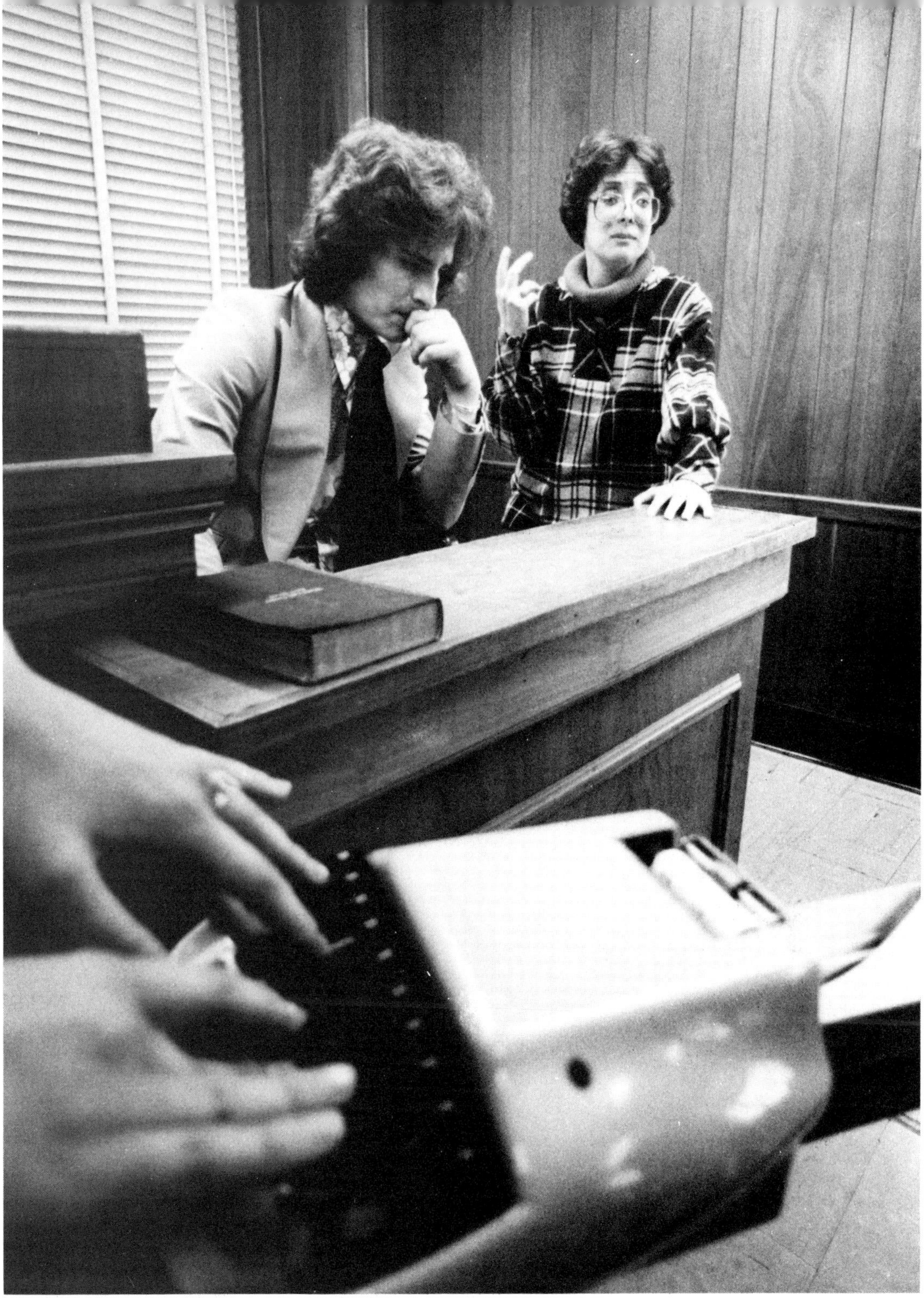

to present its case. John took the stand. Once again he testified that Laurie had suggested using Porter's car.

"Did you object at first?" asked Ms. Burns.

"Yes," said John, "but Laurie insisted."

"Did you intend to return the car?"

"Yes, right after the concert," replied John. "I know it was bad judgment to have used the car, but I intended to return it."

Then the prosecution cross-examined John.

"You admit taking the car, is that correct?" asked Armer.

"Yes," said John.

"And you drove the car. Is that correct?"

"Yes."

"And you parked the car, illegally. Is that correct?"

"Yes."

"And you were arrested while driving the car. Is that correct?"

"Yes."

"For the record, Mr. Singleton, are you admitting that you stole Mr. Porter's car?"

John felt trapped. He had not meant to steal the car. Yet Armer made it sound as if he had.

"No," he answered after a long pause. Then he added weakly, "I don't admit I stole that car."

"I have no further questions,

Your Honor," Armer said.

After the evidence had been presented, the jury went out to make its decision.

Two hours later, they were back. The jury found John guilty as charged. The judge ordered John to appear for sentencing one week later. Until then, John had to stay in jail.

It was a long week for John. He knew he might be going to prison for a year or more, and, as each day passed, the idea of prison became more frightening.

The sentence

John did not receive a year in prison. Instead he was sentenced to 60 days in the county jail followed by two years' probation. Stunned and shaking, he was taken from the courtroom by two deputies. They led him to a bus which took him to the county jail.

At the jail, John was taken to a cell. It was small, about eight by 12 feet, and it had no windows. There was a small basin, a toilet, and a small metal shelf for personal belongings. There were two metal bunks attached to the wall. A guard told John he would be allowed out of his cell a few times a week for an hour of exercise. He could make phone calls and have visitors at certain

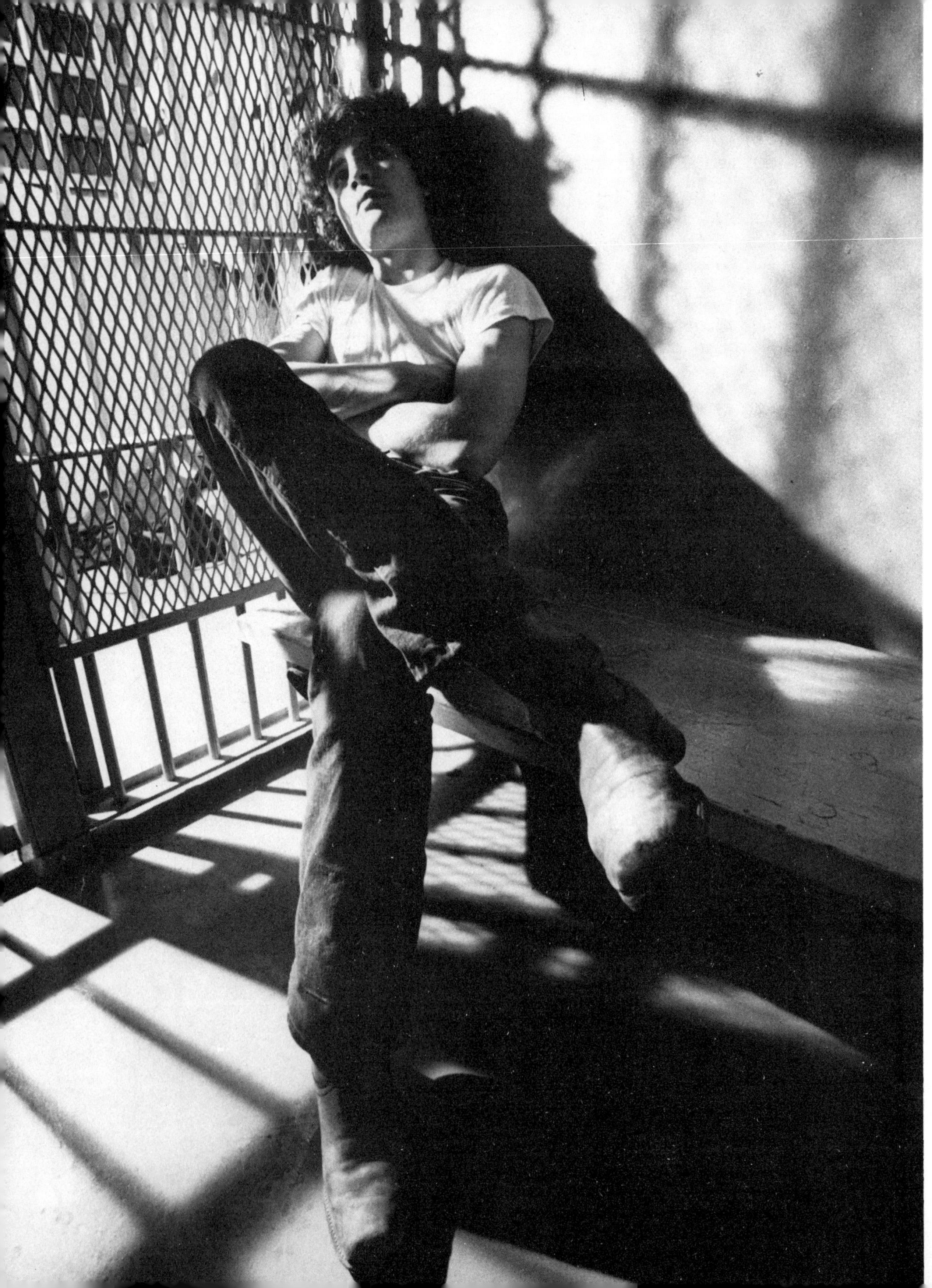

times. Twice a week, he could take a shower.

The cell was uncomfortable, and John felt very discouraged.

That night as he lay on his bunk, he could hear the sounds of prisoners snoring and the voices of deputies and new prisoners. What will happen to me now, John wondered, just before he dropped off into a troubled sleep.

Your Turn

1. In what ways were Laurie's hearing and John's trial different? Why would they differ?

2. Do you think the juvenile court judge made the right decision in Laurie's case? Did the jury make the right decision in John's case? Do you think John's sentence was fair? Give reasons for each of your answers.

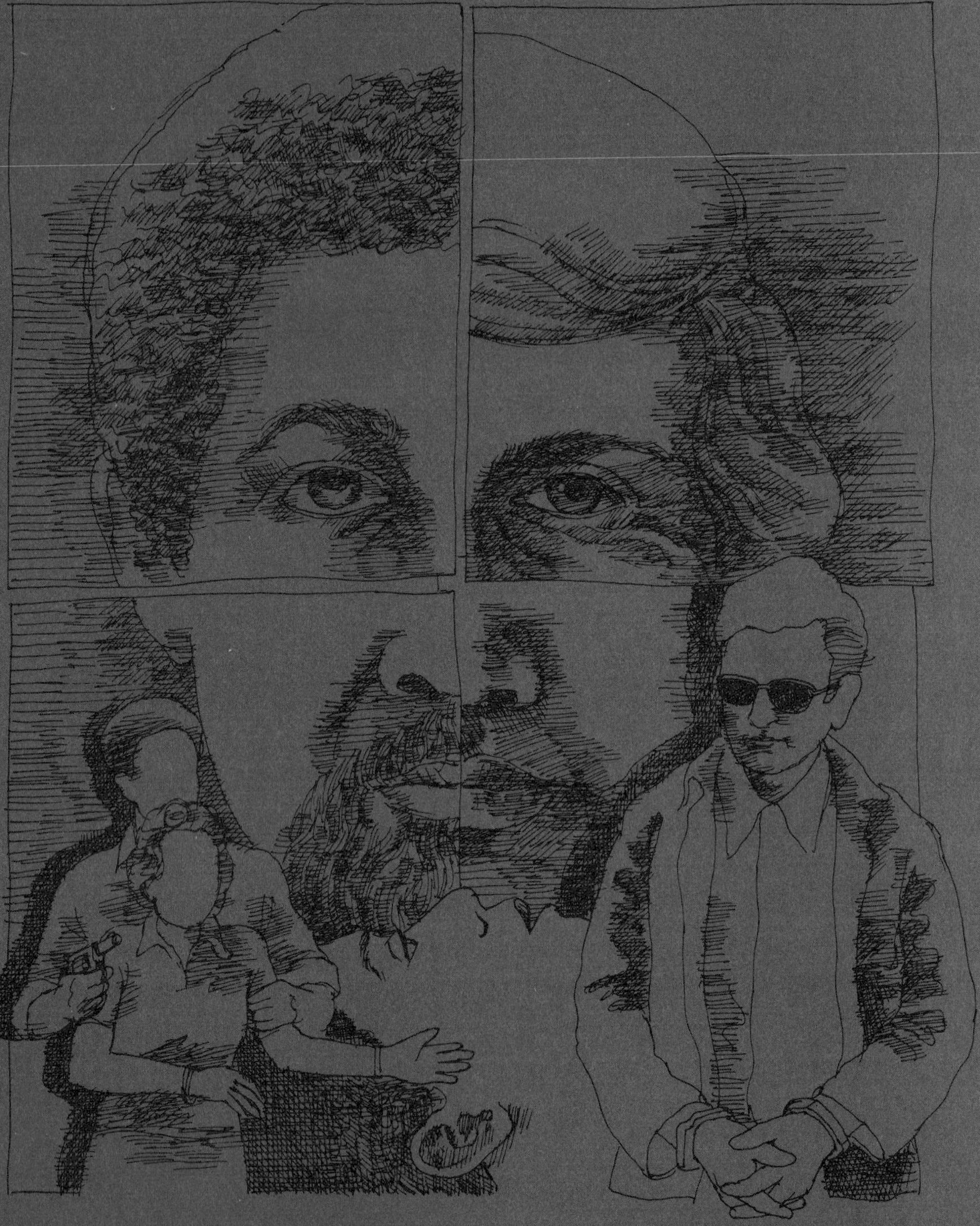

Chapter 2
Crime, Criminals, and Victims

Who are the criminals? Do they make up only a small part of our population? Or do many Americans commit criminal acts? Are criminals generally young or old? Poor or rich? Violent or nonviolent? Who is the typical American criminal? Below are four questions about criminals in the U.S. You may be surprised at the answers.

Most Americans never commit criminal acts for which they could be arrested and put on trial. True or false?

Studies have shown that most people at some point in their lives have committed acts for which they could have been arrested and put on trial — *if they had been caught.* In one survey of 1,700 people, 91 percent said that they had committed one or more acts for which they might have gone to jail. It appears that the difference between criminals and noncriminals may not be as sharp as most people think.

Which age group is most deeply involved in committing violent crimes? (a) 18–20 year olds; (b) 26–28 year olds; (c) 34–36 year olds; (d) over 40.

Violent crimes such as murder, rape, assault, and robbery are most frequently committed by young criminals. The 18–20 age group is the most deeply involved in *violent* crime. For most *property* crimes, such as burglary and theft, the age group most frequently involved is even younger: 15–17.

Which of the following applies to most people who are sentenced to prison? They (a) are male. (b) are poor. (c) grew up in broken homes. (d) have less than a high school education. (e) are unskilled. (f) are unmarried.

All are typical of people in prison in the U.S. Does this mean, then, that persons who are poor and uneducated, to take one example, are the "criminal class" of this country? Not really. The vast majority of people in this group are honest and work hard. Also, defendants who are wealthy can afford more expensive legal help for their court troubles.

Which of the following activities are generally associated with criminals involved in "organized crime"? (a) Supplying illegal goods and services to ordinary citizens. (b) Using legal businesses to cover illegal activities. (c) Using force and terror. (d) Bribing and corrupting police and other government officials.

All of the above are done by organized crime. Popular accounts often show organized crime operating only by force and terror. Actually, organized crime is also involved in many legal businesses.

1. Crime in the U.S.

A man writes a letter to his local newspaper:

"So many of my friends, neighbors, and relatives are getting mugged, stabbed, assaulted, and robbed that I know it is just a matter of days or merely hours before my turn will come.

"For the first time I know how a helpless old man, a woman, or a child feels while walking down the street in early evening darkness. Scared and helpless, with no policemen around. Knowing that no one wants to get involved."

It will come as no surprise to you that crime is a huge national problem. Poll after poll shows that Americans believe crime is one of their biggest problems—perhaps their number one problem. They have good reason to believe this. More crimes were committed in 1980 and 1981 than ever before,

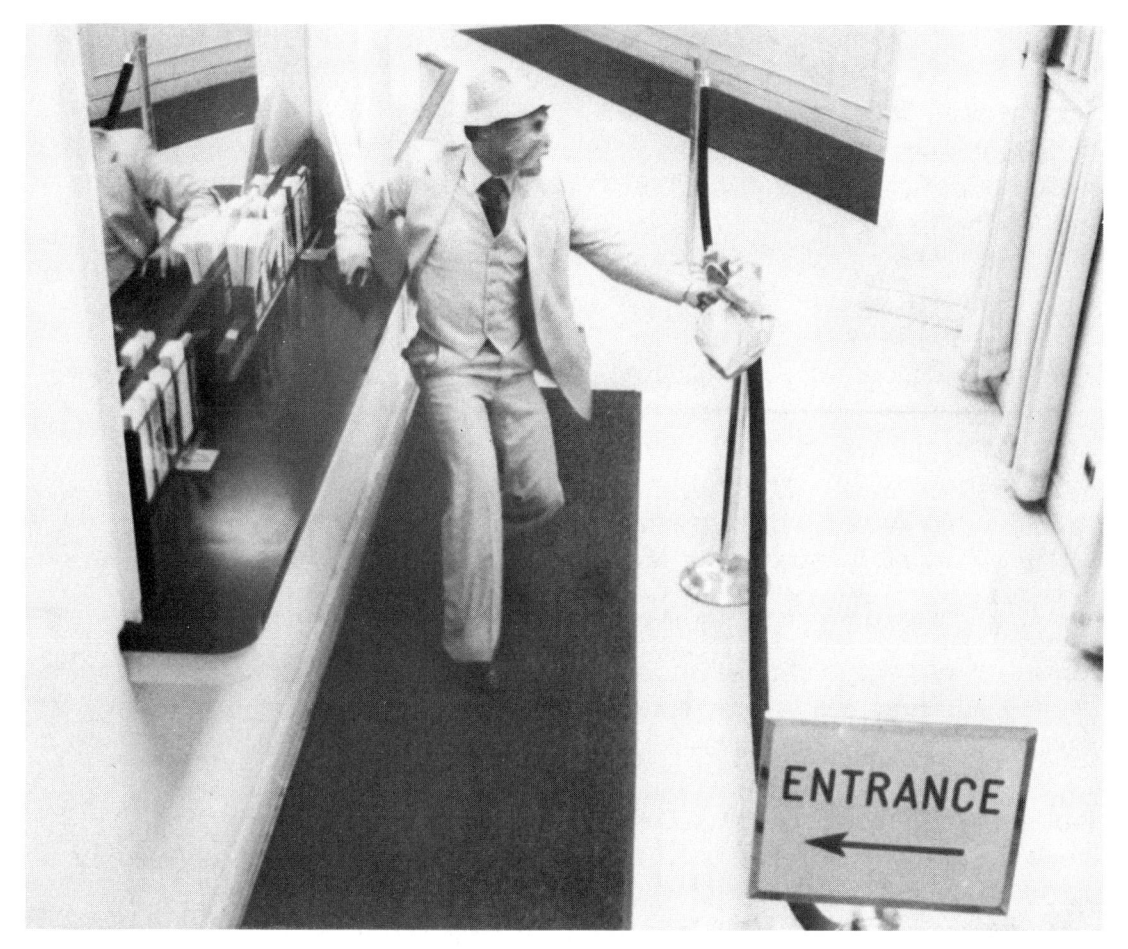

An automatic camera catches a masked robber running from a bank with gun in one hand and bag of money in the other.

acccording to FBI figures on crime rates.

Since 1981, crime has lessened a bit. The rates of serious crimes, such as murder, burglary, and armed robbery, have actually gone down. What factors might have accounted for this? Many experts point to the fact that the "baby boom" generation— the huge numbers of Americans born between 1945 and 1964—is growing older, and thus less likely to commit crimes. Other people believe that tougher prison sentences and more effective police prevention have brought down the crime rate.

37

Still, crime remains a huge problem. The overall crime rate in 1984 was *up* 5.2% over the crime rate measured just ten years before. And many people believe that crime may be on the rise again.

Cities have usually been considered the places where crime is most common. But today, crime exists everywhere—in rural areas and suburbs as well as in cities. And it deeply affects the way people live and the way they think. Many people today believe that they are not safe.

Yet we really know very little about crime. Some studies show that about three out of every four serious crimes are never reported to the police. Only about 1 in five of the 14 million crimes that are reported each year result in an arrest. Out of every 100 violent crimes committed, only two result in jail sentences. Thus it is hard to say for sure just *who* the criminals are.

But some basic facts are clear. About half of all arrests are males in their teens or early 20's. Most criminals live in cities and come from broken homes. Most have either left school or are doing very poorly at school. About 70 percent of all adults who go to prison for serious crimes have already been in jail at least once before.

Strangely enough, this description of the "typical criminal" also resembles the "typical victim" of crime. The typical victim is also male, poor, and lives in a city. The big difference is that the victim is usually an adult. The criminal is usually in his teens or early twenties.

The "white-collar criminal" does not fit this description at all. He or she has usually reached a position of trust in a business or charity. Using this position, the white-collar criminal steals funds, takes bribes, or fixes prices. In money terms, white-collar crime costs far more each year than all the violent crime combined. Estimates run as high as 200 billion dollars a year.

But it is violent crime that disturbs most Americans. Because of their fears, millions of people are demanding that something be done about crimes such as murder, assault, robbery, and burglary. They call for increased police protection and tougher measures against criminals.

Your Turn

1. How does crime affect the way we live?

2. Is crime a real threat to your way of life today? Why or why not?

Chartread: crime statistics

In the first half of the 1980's, the rates of crimes like murder, burglary, and robbery went down significantly, while crimes like assault and rape were on the increase. Chart 1 shows the increase in total crimes and in four major types of crime between 1981 and 1985. Chart 2 is based on the average number of murder victims for each 100,000 people.

What accounts for the decreasing rates for the first three crimes? One reason may be that law enforcement agencies may be getting tougher on offenders and discouraging would-be offenders. Another may be that with prison overcrowding, more felons may be allowed to plead guilty to a lesser charge in order to reduce their time in prison. There may be other reasons as well that are specific to each crime. For example, burglars may be deterred by an increase in the use of electronic security systems.

What accounts for the increasing rates for the last crime? One reason may be that law enforcement agencies are not tough enough on offenders to discourage would-be offenders. Another reason may be that more rape victims are reporting the offenses to the police. However, surveys show that even today, nearly half of all rapes go unreported.

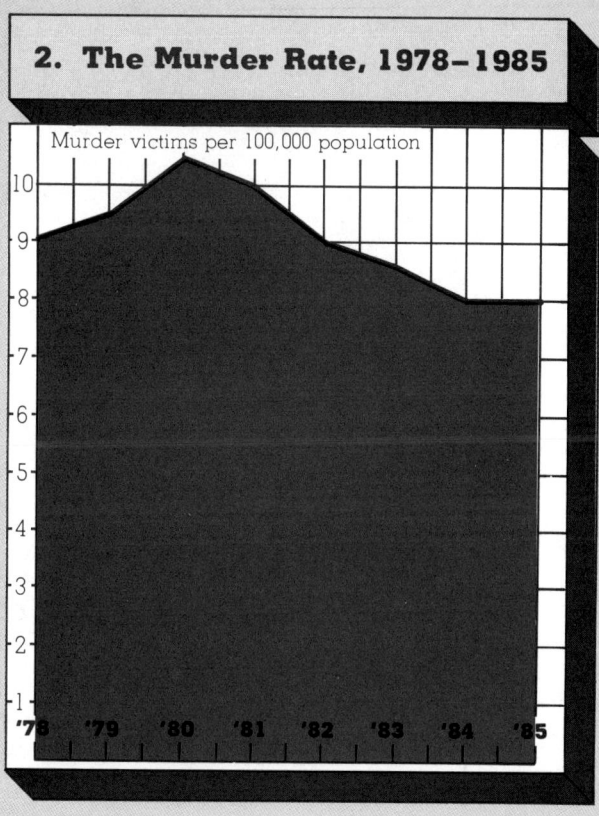

1. Total and Selected Crimes, 1981–1985

Crimes	Percent change from 1981–1985
Total crimes	down 7%
Murder	down 16%
Robbery	down 16%
Burglary	down 19%
Rape	up 6%

2. The Murder Rate, 1978–1985

Murder victims per 100,000 population

FBI Uniform Crime Reports

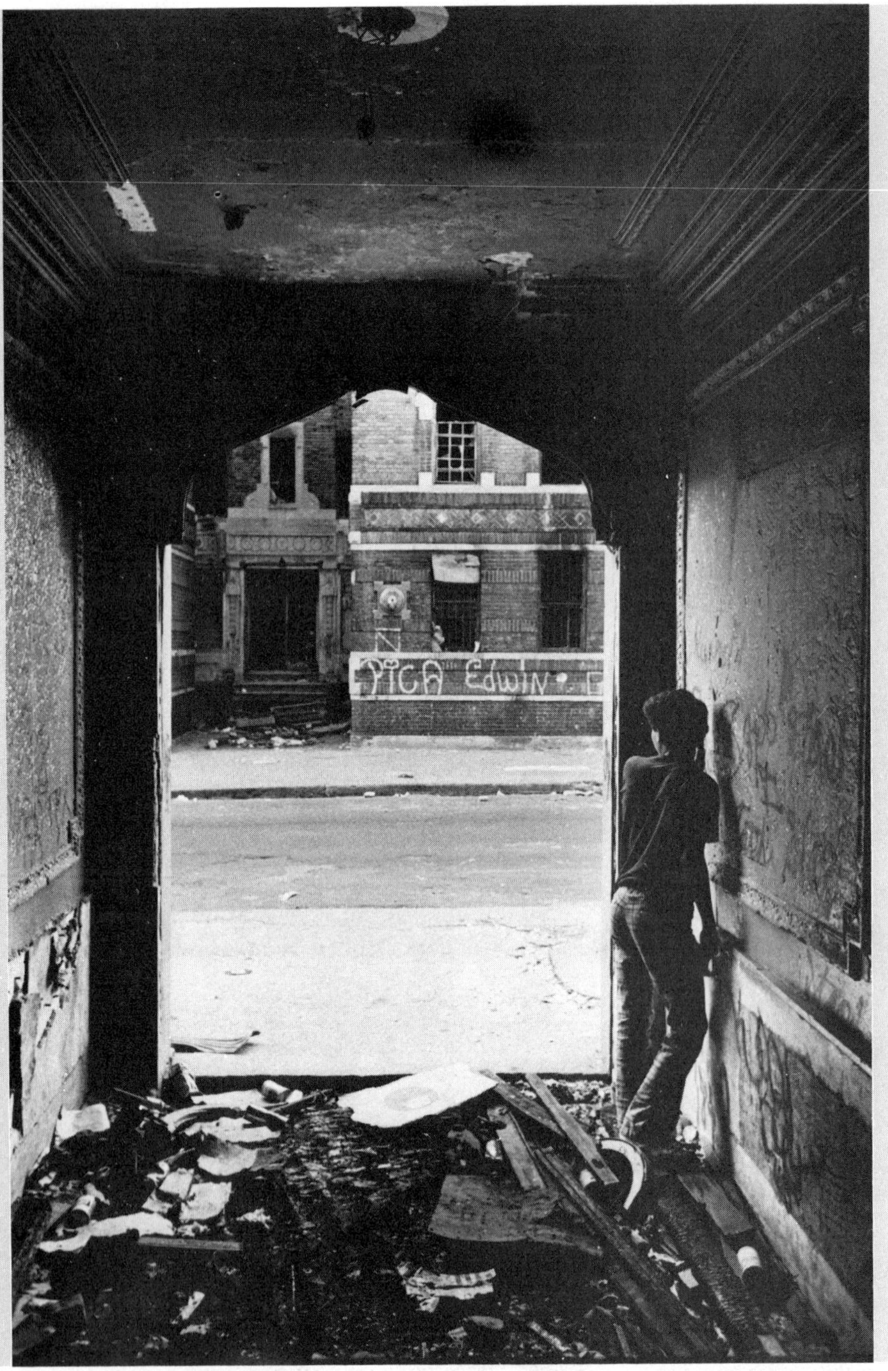
PICA Edwin

3.
What causes crime?

Experts can give many reasons why people commit crime. But no one theory is fully accepted by experts in crime control. Here are some—but not all—theories of why crime has grown so much in recent years.

Crime and poverty

Most people accept the fact that crime is somehow connected with poverty. Many studies have shown that crime is highest where incomes are lowest. These are also areas where health is poorest, unemployment is highest, and housing is oldest. The theory is that people in these areas have little "stake" in society. Some of them may feel that they have little to lose if they are arrested or jailed. A Presidential commission which studied crime in 1967 put it this way: "Warring on poverty, inadequate housing, and unemployment is warring on crime."

And yet, there is some evidence to show that poverty by itself does not cause crime. For example, the U.S. today is far wealthier than ever before in its history. Yet poorer nations than ours have far less crime. In addition, the increase in the U.S. crime rate that began in the 1960's followed almost 20 years of good times. Finally, there is a mountain of evidence to show that poor people are just as honest as anyone else. Clearly, although poverty is a factor, there are other factors also at work behind our crime rates.

More youth—more crime

The age group with the highest crime rate is made up of youths 15 to 24 years old. In 1950 there were 24 million people in this age group. Today there are more than 42 million. Since young people commit more crime than other age groups, and since there are more young people, there is bound to be more crime.

But even this simple explanation has some flaws. For crime has gone up much faster than has the number of young people. Thus, some experts look not just to the *numbers* of young people, but to the *influences* upon them.

Permissive parents

Some people believe that parents today are too permissive. That is, these parents aren't strict enough and don't teach their children to respect and obey them. In this view, such children grow up without solid values. They never learn to respect the law and the people who represent the law. Another argument is that young people who get things too easily never learn to respect the property of others.

Youth unemployment

Many people think that lack of employment contributes to crime rates. In 1984, the jobless rate for young people reached well over 20 percent. That's more than twice the rate for adults. For black youths, the statistics were even worse. For example, 42.7 percent of black males aged 16-19 were unemployed in 1984. To some experts, this mass of jobless youth is like a time bomb ready to explode.

The system

Many people believe that the rise in crime has resulted in part from the criminal justice system itself. This argument has two sides.

Some people charge that the courts are not hard enough on criminals. Critics talk of "revolving door justice." They mean that a person commits a serious crime, is caught, imprisoned for a short period of time, then released, and is free to commit another crime. If these people were imprisoned for longer terms, critics say, criminals would be kept off the streets.

On the other hand, some critics say that putting people behind bars for longer terms will not reduce crime. Some studies show that prisons may even help make criminals. People sentenced for minor crimes may become hard-core criminals in prison.

Some critics also believe that the criminal justice system is overloaded with offenses such as drunkenness and drug use. These, say the critics, are *victimless crimes*, since they hurt only the offender. Thus they should be dealt with outside the justice system. Other people disagree, saying that these crimes *do* hurt others.

As you can see, the question of what causes crime is very complex. Most likely, there are many causes. Yet it is only when we have an idea of what causes crime that we can say just what we would do about it.

Your Turn

1. Can you think of any other possible causes of crime which are not mentioned above?
2. Which of the above arguments do you think give the best reasons for the increase in crime today? Explain your answers.

4. Dilemma: shoplifting

It is natural to think of a crime as a violent act. Few of us can find anything good in an act that is both a crime *and* violent. But most crime is not violent. And sometimes nonviolent crime causes some sticky moral problems. For example, each of the following cases concerns *shoplifting*, which costs U.S. storeowners more than five billion dollars a year. Shoplifting is a crime. What would you do if you were a witness to each of the following cases?

Department store

You are in an expensive department store. You see a middle-aged, well-dressed woman slip several expensive bottles of perfume into her shopping bag. Then she walks off toward the store exit. Do you tell the salesperson what you have just seen?

Clothing store

You are in a clothing store. You look down the aisle and see a friend placing several pieces of clothing into a bag. Which of the following actions do you take? (a) Do nothing. (b) Tell a salesperson. (c) Try to persuade your friend to return the clothing. (d) Tell your parents. (e) Tell the parents of your friend. (f) Some other action.

Supermarket

You are shopping for groceries in a supermarket. As you move up one aisle, you notice a woman and two small children walking toward you. The woman is pushing a market basket with a crying baby inside. You see that they all are wearing old worn clothes. The children are very thin and look hungry. The woman seems to cough a lot. As you shop, you see the woman several times slipping some canned food into a bag she is carrying. What do you do?

Your Turn

1. What do the three cases have in common? How do they differ?

2. Have you been consistent in deciding what you would do about each case? Or do your reactions depend on the different circumstances? Are you satisfied with your reactions? Why or why not?

3. Assume that all of the shoplifters in the above situations were arrested, brought to trial, and found guilty. Now suppose that you are the judge who is to sentence them. What kind of sentence would you give each shoplifter? (a) A fine. (b) Jail. (c) A suspended jail sentence (which would be imposed if the defendant shoplifted again). (d) Other.

Field Activity

Crime in America: an opinion poll

A good way to find out where people in your school and community stand on the crime problem is through an opinion poll. A good opinion poll is made up of some carefully worded questions. These questions force people to take a clear position on some issues. You and your classmates can make up your own questions about crime. You can give the poll in your own class, in other classes, and among adults. You can then compare results from your class with those of other classes.

The first step, and the hardest, is to come up with some interesting questions. To get started, look over the following questions.

Gun Control

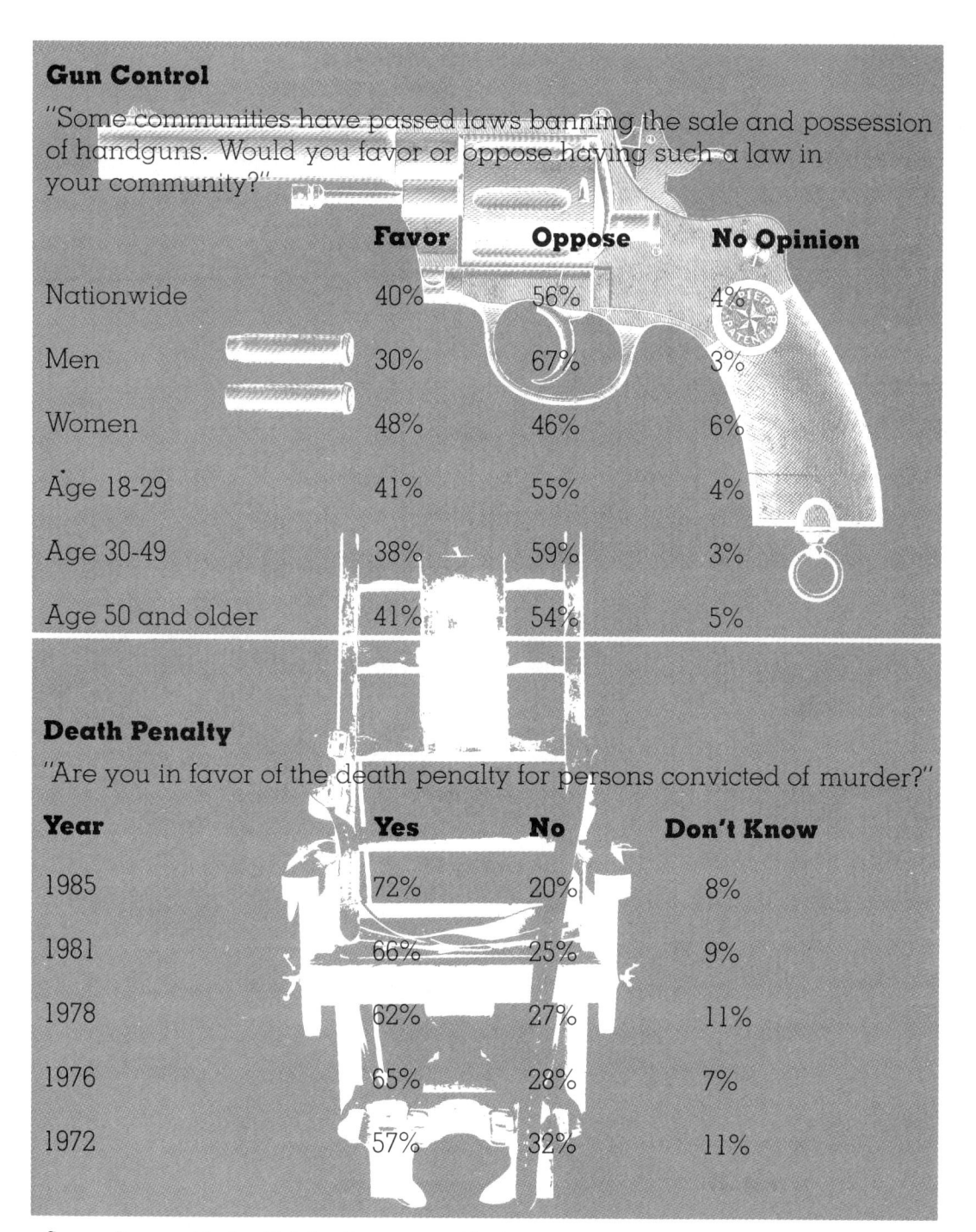

"Some communities have passed laws banning the sale and possession of handguns. Would you favor or oppose having such a law in your community?"

	Favor	Oppose	No Opinion
Nationwide	40%	56%	4%
Men	30%	67%	3%
Women	48%	46%	6%
Age 18-29	41%	55%	4%
Age 30-49	38%	59%	3%
Age 50 and older	41%	54%	5%

Death Penalty

"Are you in favor of the death penalty for persons convicted of murder?"

Year	Yes	No	Don't Know
1985	72%	20%	8%
1981	66%	25%	9%
1978	62%	27%	11%
1976	65%	28%	7%
1972	57%	32%	11%

Source: Bureau of Justice Statistics, Department of Justice

Student-made opinion poll

The following questions were developed by high school students in Los Angeles. The poll was given to students in several junior high classes. About 500 junior high students answered the questions. Because this poll was taken in a limited number of junior high schools, we cannot be sure these are the true opinions of most Los Angeles junior high students.

	Yes	No
1 Do you feel that marijuana should be made legal?	49%	51%
2 Do you feel that high school students should be allowed to smoke tobacco on school grounds?	35%	65%
3 Are you generally satisfied with the job police are doing in your community?	34%	66%
4 Do you feel safe walking the streets in your neighborhood at night?	77%	23%
5 Do you feel that police should have the right to ask you personal questions?	35%	65%

Peer teaching the crime survey

The ideas and views you have received during the crime poll can be shared with other students. This process of sharing your knowledge with other young people is called *peer teaching*. (The word "peer" in this case means "equal" or "on the same level.")

The idea of shifting from learner to teacher may scare you a bit. However, you will probably find that once you do it, you enjoy it. You do not have to be a "whiz kid" in school to peer teach. But you will have to do some planning and preparing. Your teacher can help you with your planning.

The crime survey can be used for peer teaching. With the permission and help of your teacher, you can peer teach a lesson dealing with the crime poll. Throughout the rest of this book, we will point out lessons which you can use to teach others.

Chapter 3
The Law

One person living alone — a hermit, perhaps — can get along pretty well without laws. But put two or more people together, and sooner or later they will disagree on something. They will disagree not because they are bad, but because they are different.

Laws are meant to limit these disputes. All societies in the world have some system of law. Laws are quite different from place to place and from time to time. Yet the need for law seems to be basic to human life. This chapter explores the reasons why laws exist. It also discusses how laws come about and how they change. It defines the two major branches of law — civil law and criminal law — and it gives you the chance to decide if a number of situations come under civil or criminal law.

A few LINES on
Magnus Mode, Richard Hodges & J. Newington Clark.
Who are Sentenc'd to stand one Hour in the
Pillory at Charlestown;
To have one of their EARS cut off, and to be Whipped 20 Stripes at the public Whipping-Post, for making and passing Counterfeit DOLLARS, &c.

In colonial America, punishment was harsh by today's standards. Top, a Massachusetts criminal is put in pillory. According to notice, he will then be publicly whipped and have an ear cut off. Below, the dunking stool was a common punishment in many colonies.

1.
Why do we need laws?

At one time or another, we all get into arguments. At home we may argue over the use of the TV, over whose turn it is to wash the dishes, or who left the water on and flooded the bathroom.

We get into disputes outside the home too. Two neighbors may argue because a dog belonging to one of them barks all night long and keeps the other awake. Or two drivers in an auto accident may disagree over who is at fault.

This is one reason we have laws: *to help settle disputes.* Another reason we have laws is *to protect the general welfare.* For example, we have laws to prevent factories from dumping poisons into a town's water supply. We have laws *to help set safety standards.* For example, buildings must meet fire safety standards. We have laws *to keep us healthy.* For example, foods must meet certain standards of quality before they are sold.

A law defines how to behave. It tells you precisely what to do — or what not to do. It also tells you what to expect if you do not obey the law. Clearly, not all laws are good. A law can be very unjust and very harmful. But when people know how they are expected to behave and what to expect from others, fewer disagreements arise. When disagreements and conflict do arise, laws give us a way to reach a settlement.

Why do laws change?

Laws give you a good picture of the values of a society. Sometimes a law that seems fair at one period of time seems harsh in another period. For example, our attitudes toward crime and law change constantly.

As late as the early 19th century in Britain and the U.S., children were punished just as harshly as adults. A boy of eight was hanged for burning two barns. A boy of 10 was hanged for killing his friend. A servant girl of 13 was burned at the stake for killing her mistress. Youths were also thrown into the same prison as adults. But by the middle of the 19th century, both Britain and the U.S. began to treat youths and adults differently.

Today there are juvenile courts and corrections systems in Britain and in every U.S. state. But now, some attitudes toward juvenile justice are again changing. The quick rise in juvenile crime has led many people to call for much harsher penalties for young

Changing ideas about punishment. Inmates in a reform school a century ago.

criminals. Some people even say that young people who commit serious crimes should be treated just the same as adults.

Because society changes, ideas about fairness and justice change. And then laws change.

2. Law and daily life

Few people realize how nearly everything we do in our daily lives is affected in some way by law. Laws affect birth, marriage, education, business, employment, housing, illness, traffic, food, retirement, death, to name a few. Laws affect the person who obeys the law as well as the criminal. It may surprise you just how much influence law has on your life. List everything you have done in the past 24 hours. How many actions were influenced by law? For example, what time did you get up this morning? Was it influenced by the law which says you must attend school? Now what about eating breakfast, walking to school, crossing the street, driving a car, buying food, watching television?

Civil and criminal law

In the American legal system, there are two basic types of law: *civil* law and *criminal* law. In general, civil laws govern our private lives and private businesses. For example, most laws dealing with family relations, such as birth, adoption, marriage, and divorce are civil laws. Other civil laws deal with private matters such as business contracts — for example, an agreement to buy a car on the installment plan.

Civil laws also deal with injuries and damages caused by accidents. For example, a person injured in an auto accident may believe another person caused the accident. The other person may disagree. If the injured person makes a civil complaint, the court must decide who is right. However, the person who is judged guilty does not go to jail. He or she may be required to pay a sum of money to the person who wins the case. (For more on civil law, see *Civil Justice* in the LIVING LAW PROGRAM.)

Criminal laws, on the other hand, deal with crimes. In this book, you will study criminal law. A crime is considered a public matter. That is, although there may be one victim, or many victims, the state views the crime as an offense against society. Thus it is not the victim or victims who bring a criminal case to court. (Victims may, however, bring a separate civil suit against the accused person.) Instead, action in

A criminal case is begun by government officials representing society as a whole.

Criminal laws usually describe the acts that are crimes. They also state how such acts will be punished. Punishment is usually a term in a prison or a fine or both. When someone is fined for a criminal act, the fine is paid to the government, not to the victim.

Your Turn

Read the six statements below. Does each statement refer to a civil law or a criminal law?

• If you damage someone's property with your car during an accident, you must pay him or her for the damage.

• If you use your car to purposely kill someone, you may be charged with murder.

• If you wish to marry, you must take a blood test and then obtain a marriage license.

• If you are married to more than one person at a time, you may be charged with bigamy.

• If you take a loan to buy a car and fail to pay back the bank, the car may be taken from you.

• If someone promises to put a new roof on your house and then takes your money and disappears, that person may be charged with theft.

Chapter 4
Criminal Law and the Bill of Rights

Americans have certain basic rights as citizens. These are sometimes called civil rights. They are described in the Bill of Rights, the first 10 amendments to the U.S. Constitution. In general, the Bill of Rights protects Americans from their government. Many of these rights are practiced by Americans in their ordinary everyday life. For example, sections of the Bill of Rights deal with the rights of Americans to practice freedom of the press, religion, and free speech.

But certain of the rights deal with people in a special situation: those who have been accused of a crime. Many of the first 10 amendments are concerned with making sure that an accused person will be treated fairly. It is these rights that are the focus of this chapter.

The fictionalized story which follows shows what things might be like without the U.S. Bill of Rights.

1.
An enemy of the people

Dick Lambert was on his way home. He had just made a speech to a crowd of 200 people in the park. He had asked them to elect him mayor in the election next week. "I stand for good, honest government and the right of the people to elect their leaders in open elections. Right now, our government is dishonest and threatens our rights."

When he got home, Dick noticed his front door was open. "I thought I had locked that door," Dick said to himself. As he drew closer, he saw why his door was open. Someone had used an ax to force the lock. Inside, Dick found his belongings and papers thrown about. He heard voices in the basement.

"Who's there?" he asked with some fear. It was the police. They were searching his house. Dick asked them for their warrant, but they laughed. "Richard Lambert," said a policeman, "you are under arrest by order of the mayor."

"What's the charge?" Dick asked. "Why am I being arrested?"

"You'll find out later," the officer answered.

Lambert was taken to the police

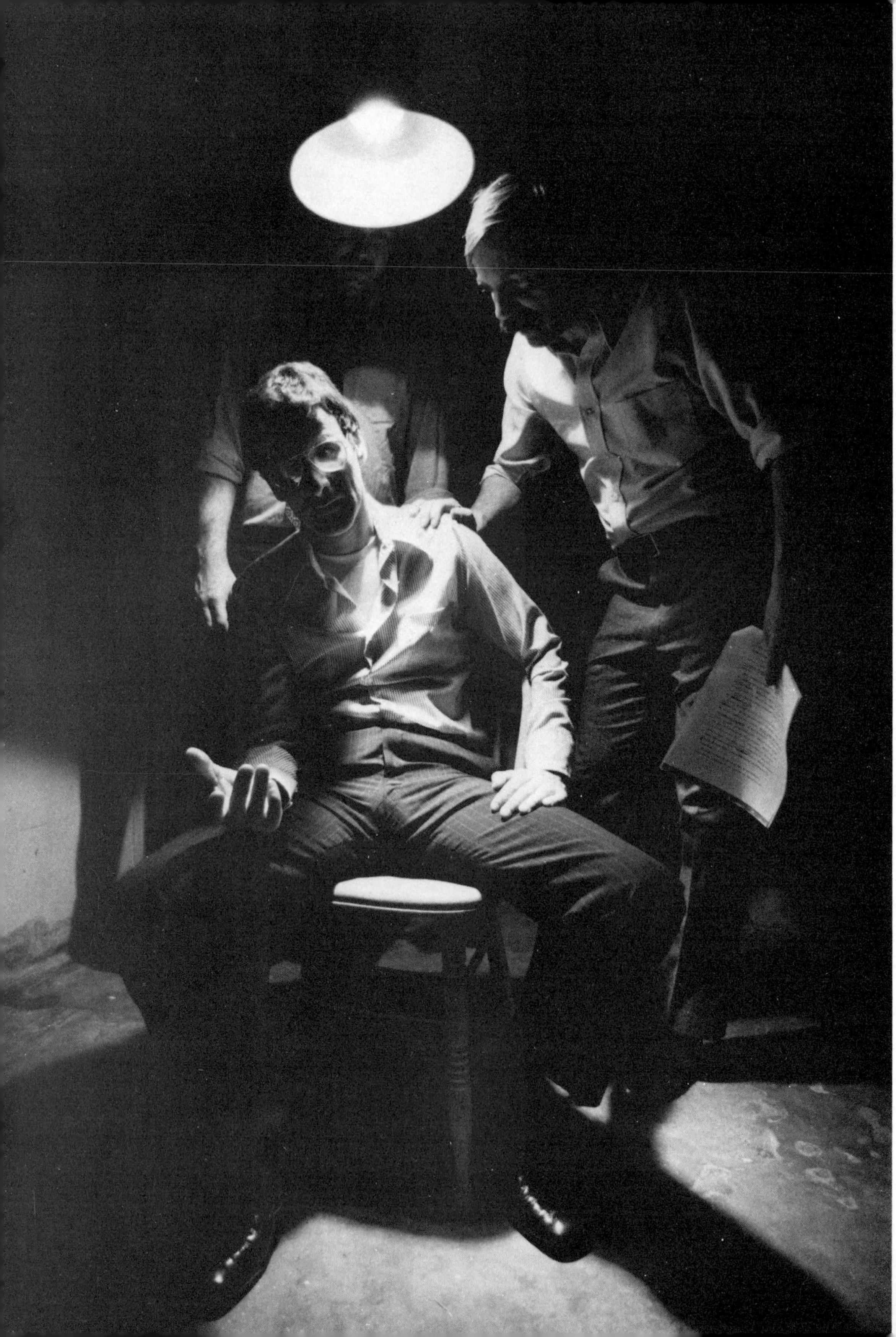

station and kept there for a few weeks. He was not informed of the charge against him. He was not allowed to see a lawyer. He was questioned over and over again for long hours. He was threatened. Finally, he was brought to trial.

It was very brief. Several people stated that Dick had spoken against the government. Others said that Dick had tried to stir up a riot. A prosecutor waved some papers and said, "Your Honor, these papers are so secret I cannot read them in public. I ask you to look at them in private. You will see that Richard Lambert is guilty of disrespect for the government."

The judge accepted the papers and went to his chambers. Later that day he returned to the courtroom and announced that he had found Dick guilty. "Richard Lambert, you are an enemy of the people. I sentence you to three years in prison at hard labor." No reporters were allowed at the trial. No witnesses were allowed to appear on Dick's behalf. No appeal was permitted.

Dick Lambert was led away. The next day, the mayor's office announced that because Dick Lambert had been found guilty of a crime, he would not be allowed to run in the election. The mayor won the election with 95 percent of the votes. Several weeks later, after the election, Dick Lambert was released from prison.

The Bill of Rights
This story is fictional. It did not happen here — or anywhere else for that matter. In the United States, the Bill of Rights outlaws many of the things that happened to Dick Lambert. Of course, it is not the Bill of Rights alone which protects us. Americans believe strongly in the Bill of Rights and are willing to support and fight for it. Without that support, the Bill of Rights would be just a scrap of paper.

The Bill of Rights protects Americans against unfair laws and unfair acts of government. Below is a list of protections in the Bill of Rights. Not all these protections are stated in so many words. It is the job of the U.S. Supreme Court to interpret these rights in the light of today's conditions. And over the years the Supreme Court has ruled that we do have many protections because of general statements in the Bill of Rights.

 a. Americans have the right to criticize elected officials.

 b. Newspapers have the right to cover almost all news stories that they think are important, without being censored by government.

 c. Except in very limited cases, police must have search warrants issued by a judge in order to search a private house or office.

 d. Americans have the right *not* to be kept in jail for long periods of time before being brought to trial.

 e. Americans have the right to call on their government to change its policies.

 f. Americans have the right to demonstrate peacefully against the government without interference from the police.

 g. Americans have the right to practice their religious beliefs without government interference.

 h. Americans who are arrested have the right to call for immediate help from a lawyer.

 i. Americans have the right to refuse to answer questions from the police about a crime for which they have been arrested.

 j. Americans have the right to be told why they have been arrested.

Rights of the accused
The Constitution and the Bill of Rights protect everybody, not just people we like or agree with. Some of the most important sections protect people who are

The witch trials which took place in Salem, Massachusetts, in the 17th century were a good example of what can happen when people accused of crimes are denied their basic rights.

accused of crimes. These protections are aimed at making sure that all citizens are treated fairly by police, courts, and prisons. All Americans have the right to a lawyer, the right to a fair trial, and the right to receive just punishment if found guilty. Here is a list of those rights from the Constitution and the Bill of Rights that form the basis for our criminal justice system.

Habeas corpus. This is a part of Article I of the Constitution. It says that authorities cannot arrest and hold a person without saying why and where he is being held. If a judge feels that there is no good reason for holding the prisoner, he must be released. This keeps the government from secretly arresting persons. Article I also outlaws *ex post facto* laws.

Ex post facto. An ex post facto

law is one which outlaws an act after it has happened. For example, say you are arrested for speeding in a 55-mile-per-hour zone. You were driving at only 50 mph. The day after your arrest, the law is changed so that the speed limit is lowered to 40 miles per hour. You cannot be punished for having broken this new law.

Fourth Amendment. Among other things, this prevents the police from "*unreasonable* search and seizure." Usually the police must have a search warrant, issued by a judge. (For more on search and seizure, see Chapter Six.)

Fifth Amendment. This gives a person accused of a serious crime the right to a hearing by a grand jury (see page 112) before a trial can be held. The grand jury must decide if there is enough evidence to hold a trial. The same amendment gives people the right not to be forced to *incriminate* themselves. This means that people do not have to answer questions or give evidence which might later be used against them in a criminal proceeding. The federal government also cannot try a person twice for the same crime. This is called "double jeopardy." Finally, Americans have the right not to lose "life, liberty, or property, without *due process* of law." (For more on due process, see page 114.)

Sixth Amendment. This amendment states that a person accused of a crime must get a speedy and public trial and that the jury must be fair. An accused person has the right to a lawyer. That person also has the right to question witnesses who give testimony against him and to get witnesses who will support him. (For more on the Sixth Amendment, see pages 88–95.)

Eighth Amendment. This bars excessive bail and fines. It also bars "cruel and unusual punishments." (For more on bail, see page 115.)

At first, the Bill of Rights limited acts of the federal government only. But later, the Supreme Court ruled that many parts of the Bill of Rights apply to state and local government too.

The section above is only an outline of these rights. Later in this book, you will see in detail how our criminal justice system must balance society's need to protect itself against criminals with the right of citizens to be free from government interference.

Your Turn

Which of Dick Lambert's rights were violated by the government?

Crime and the System: a Bibliography

Crime and Justice in Our Time
by Margaret O'Hyde, Franklin Watts, 1983.
An overview of the U.S. criminal justice system. It covers the debate on the causes of crime.

Fahrenheit 451
by Ray Bradbury, Ballantine Books, 1981.
A science-fiction story about a society in which all activities are controlled by the state. The central character is a fireman whose job is to burn books. While doing this, he becomes interested in the books. Thus he becomes an enemy of the state.

Lord of the Flies
by William Golding, Coward-McCann, 1978.
A group of boys marooned on an island create their own society. As their primitive instincts emerge, their respect for law crumbles.

The Ox Bow Incident
by Walter Van Tilburg Clark, New American Library, 1972.
A posse hunting for rustlers finds three men it thinks are the criminals and proceeds to try them. This novel not only holds you in its grip. It also says a lot about due process, law and order, and capital punishment.

Thinking About Crime
by James Q. Wilson, Random House, 1977.
This is a challenging and sometimes difficult book. But it attacks a number of widely held views about the nature of crime. Wilson believes that too much attention has been paid to the causes of crime and not enough to the role of courts and parole boards in returning dangerous criminals to the streets.

PART 2
THE BADGE

Police in Our Society

Chapter 5
Behind the Badge

The scene is a high school classroom. A police officer is telling students what it is really like to be "behind the badge." The following exchange takes place between the police officer and the students.

POLICE OFFICER: This guy turned at us swinging a knife. He came close to me, but I didn't want to shoot him. Then he ran back into the bedroom and grabbed this shotgun off the wall. I knew it was empty, but the other cop didn't. The guy racked it and said, "All right, deal with this!" Now if you were a cop, what would you do?

FIRST STUDENT: I would have shot him.

POLICE OFFICER: I'll tell you something. When you rack a shotgun and it's not loaded, it has a tinny sound. When it has a live round in there, it has a harder, duller sound. So I yelled to my partner, "It's empty!" My partner grabbed the barrel of the shotgun, turned it around, and smacked him on the side of his head.

SECOND STUDENT: What happened to the knife?

POLICE OFFICER: After my partner hit him, he fell back head first into the bedroom. Then he got up and came at us again with his knife. We got the mattress off the bed and squeezed him up against the corner. My partner had gloves on, so he grabbed the knife by the blade and took it out of the guy's hand. Then we handcuffed him.

THIRD STUDENT: Why didn't you shoot him when he started to come at you with his knife?

POLICE OFFICER: You have to use your judgment. You can't grab your gun every time you feel threatened. A cop has to think on his feet, and do it quickly.

Your Turn

1. What were the two main aims of the police officers in this incident? Did those aims conflict? If so, in what way?

2. "You can't grab your gun every time you feel threatened." Explain.

3. What does this incident tell you about police work? What does it tell you about the qualities that make a good police officer?

Think fast!

How would you handle each of the following situations? There is no right or wrong answer to each case. Instead, you must use your best judgment, or *discretion*, as an officer. Break up the class into four or five discussion groups and make a decision for each of the situations. Then compare your group's decisions with those of the other groups.

• You spot two teenagers carrying spray paint cans next to a school. It is 9 P.M. Would you (a) stop and warn them? (b) scare them by pretending to arrest them? (c) take them to their parents? (d) arrest them and take them to the police station? (e) ignore the situation? (f) do something else? (If so, what?)

• You have been called to a store where a young girl has been caught shoplifting some cheap clothes. The girl tells you that this is the first time she has ever done such a thing. She pleads with you to let her go. Would you (a) ignore the young girl's plea and arrest her? (b) check out her story before arresting her? (c) release her? (d) ask the store manager what he or she thinks should be done? (e) take the shoplifter to her home and talk with her parents? (f) do something else? (If so, what?)

- You receive a call about a fight in a family. When you arrive, you find a father beating his 14-year-old son with a heavy belt. Would you (a) back off because it is none of your business? (b) restrain the father, using force if necessary? (c) try to convince the father not to beat his son? (d) arrest the father for child abuse? (e) take the son into protective custody? (f) do something else? (If so, what?)

1.
The job of the police

A police officer has two main jobs. The officer must first enforce the law. And the officer must maintain order. The two jobs may seem pretty much the same. Law and order seem to go together almost like bacon and eggs. But there are important differences, and the two roles of the police officer do not always match. Keeping order often puts the officer right into the personal disputes of citizens — a family quarrel, for example. It seldom leads to an arrest. Enforcing the law, however, usually involves the officer with lawbreakers. And of course, when lawbreaking is involved, the goal is usually arrest.

Police officers in the U.S. have long tried to play these two roles; but not always equally. For much of our early history, the emphasis was mostly on maintaining order. Enforcing the law took a backseat. Our first police were not paid, professional officers. Large towns and cities had forces of volunteers who protected the streets at night only. These forces were known as the *nightwatch*. Smaller towns and farm areas had no police force at all.

When it came to catching criminals, the nightwatch left something to be desired. In fact, the men of the nightwatch often went out of their way to avoid meeting criminals. Sometimes, they carried rattles or noisemakers to warn criminals that they were coming. It has been said of these patrols that they were "all shiver and shake." The men shivered half the night from the cold. They shook the other half from fear.

England was the first country to have a paid police force. Sir

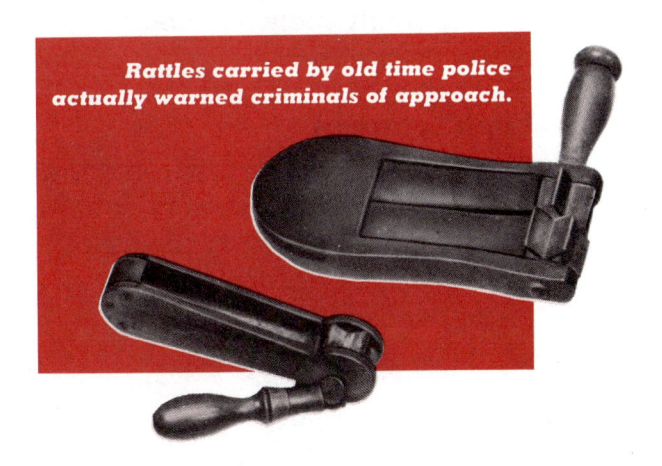

Rattles carried by old time police actually warned criminals of approach.

Robert Peel created this force in London in 1829. In his honor, the London police have since been called "Bobbies."

A few years later, a full-time police force was set up in New York. Then one was formed in Boston. By 1870 most American cities had small police forces. Even then, there was not much law enforcement. Police officers were usually hired on the basis of political influence. It wasn't until much later that police hiring was taken out of politics. When candidates were made to take tests of ability, police forces began catching criminals.

Local control

American police are different from police in other countries in one key way. In most other countries, the police are organized in one large police force run by the national government. In the U.S., there are many different police forces — about 40,000 of them, in fact. There are local police in villages, towns, cities, and counties. There are state police — the state troopers we see on the highways. There are also a number of different police groups in the federal government, for example, the FBI and the Secret Service.

Why so many police forces? Because most Americans believe that their local communities should control their police. Americans fear that a national police force might have too much power and could destroy our democracy. On the other hand, local police are easier to control. People feel it is easier to know what local police are doing.

But having 40,000 different police forces in the U.S. also has many disadvantages. There are no common standards of training, hiring, or pay. Some cases involve many different police forces. Sometimes it is hard for the different forces to work together. Also, it is more costly to run many separate small police forces than a single large one. Thus people are likely to pay more in taxes for the protection of their community.

The policeman's lot

It's hard not to have strong feelings one way or the other about the police. After all, they carry guns and clubs, and they can — and sometimes do — tell us what to do. Enforcing the law can be a pretty rough job. Some officers get killed in the process.

Yet city police say a good 80 percent of all their calls are to settle family quarrels. In small towns, most of a police officer's time may be spent directing traffic or checking out homes or businesses. It's far from nonstop excitement and danger. It's often hours of routine work. But the possibility of danger and excitement is always there.

Your Turn

What are the advantages of local control of police forces? What are the disadvantages? Can you suggest any ways in which the disadvantages might be lessened?

2.
Justice system interview: on patrol

At various points in this book you will find interviews with people who work in the criminal justice system. The interviewer was journalist Nancy Boyarsky. She spent a number of months "learning how the system works, how all the parts fit together."

Bill, the sheriff's deputy, is tall, chunky, and has short hair. He has a badge, a gun, a wooden club, and handcuffs hanging from his belt.

As we get into the squad car, I notice how well equipped it is. There is a rifle under the front seat, a two-way radio, a screen between the back of the car and the front, and a big metal box with extra handcuffs, tools, and emergency equipment. As we drive, I ask some questions.

He tells me he is a college graduate, a music major. Does the sheriff's department care what he studied? No, a college degree is not even required. Just a high school diploma. But the sheriff tries to help his men get a college degree. The deputy is paid about $2,000 a month, plus overtime. That is about $300 more than if he had no college degree.

Why police work?

First, Bill had wanted to teach. But he changed his mind in his last year of college. "I was dating a girl whose dad was a lieutenant in the homicide section. He got to talking to me and got me interested in police work. I was impressed with the officers I met who worked with him.

"There aren't many jobs where you're free. Like right now, I'm free, within certain limits, to investigate what I want and learn. It's a learning process. The guy who trained me had been in the department for 12 years. He told me, 'You're out there every day, and if you don't learn something every day, you haven't been trying.' You'll never know it all. There are 10 different ways to handle every situation."

What kinds of situations does Bill run into? "Everything," he says. "Since I've been working this car, I've had everything from a missing child to a stray sheep.

"Then you get things that everybody thinks about when you think of police work. Shootings, stabbings, that sort of thing. But there's not that much on the job."

He is called out to two auto accidents in a row. He speeds along, going through red lights. I ask why he does not use his siren. He explains he can only do that when the dispatcher says he can. Neither accident is bad. At one, a man has a broken arm, but the fire department rescue squad is already there putting it in a splint. The other accident is just a bashed-in auto fender. Each driver says it is the other's fault. The deputy tells me that no one could tell who was at fault, since the cars have pulled into a gas station. "Let their insurance companies settle it," he says. But he still must write out a report.

Dangerous work

Between accidents we talk about what the deputy worries about most in his work. First, Bill says, is his own safety. It is dangerous to work in a one-man car. "There are a lot of people who don't like you, and you don't know who they are. You can't stop somebody from getting you. It happens."

The other things that worry Bill are young people and the increase in crime among them. "Most of my arrests are minors. Most aren't arrested for just curfew violations or being truants, either. I'm talking about assault with a deadly weapon, drugs, burglary, battery . . . serious crimes where other people are hurt. I wish I had a solution to the problem.

"My role in the justice system," he says, "is in a way acting like a judge. For example, I can decide *not* to arrest somebody or give them a ticket. Suppose I get a call from, say, a neighborhood market. They have a nine-year-old boy who's stolen a candy bar. That's petty theft. And it's a crime. But we don't take nine-year-old kids to jail and we don't book them. If children are under 14, we can't treat them like criminals or even like juvenile delinquents. But, if the store insists, we detain the child and release him to his parents. A report is written.

"I could say to the store owner, 'He's a thief. I think you ought to write up a report to give him a record.' Or, I can say, 'Why don't you let me take him home to his folks. It was a small item. I can scare him and explain to his folks why he's being brought home by a police officer. I'll see what their reaction is.' That's usually what I try to do if it's a minor offense and the kid is under 14 years old."

Handling a young shoplifter

The next call is from a big department store where the store detective is holding a young shoplifter. We pull up to the store, and the deputy parks in a no-parking zone. "This isn't to save a walk," he says. "I'll have to handcuff the kid and I think it's unkind to parade him across the parking lot."

Inside, we go to the office of the store detective. Sitting by the desk is a tearful, skinny boy who is about 12 or 13. He looks very upset. The store detective tells us the boy was caught stealing a pair of sunglasses. The detective and the deputy walk into another room. The detective explains that he has tried to call the boy's parents to send him home, but they are out. The two plan how the deputy will handcuff and pretend to arrest the boy. Instead, he will stop by the boy's house first and leave him off if either parent is now home. We do just that.

The boy lives in a two-story house in a very pleasant neighborhood. The deputy rings the bell and disappears into the house. The boy is sniffling in the backseat. After a few minutes, the father and the deputy come out. The boy is told he's being released to his father. The deputy tells them that the store doesn't want the boy back again — ever.

Afterward, the deputy explains to me why he handcuffed a person who is too young and frail to be any danger. "He's in my custody, so if he should get hurt or try to escape or something like that, I've covered myself. Also, being handcuffed is very scary. Given the age of the kid and the fact that it was a small amount and they had never caught him before, I could see where justice would be served by the parent."

Your Turn

1. How did the deputy handle the shoplifting incident? Do you think this would be effective? Why or why not?

2. What does the sheriff's deputy like most about his job? What does he like least? How would you feel about the different aspects of police work?

3. Make a list of 10 police calls you think a police officer might have to respond to during a daytime shift in your area. Compare your list with those of your classmates. Do you think your list is realistic?

Field Activity

You can use this lesson in combination with a field activity in which you ride along with a law enforcement officer during his or her normal patrol. Also, you might invite a law enforcement officer to visit the class to discuss his or her work and answer some of the following questions:

1. Why did you go into police work?

2. How is your time spent? How much of it is spent solving crimes? How much of it is spent helping people with problems that don't involve crime?

3. What are the hiring requirements of your department?

4. What problems in police work worry you most?

5. What part of the job do you enjoy the most?

Chapter 6
The Police and Privacy

- The police see a number of known burglars carrying bulky boxes and pillow cases into an apartment house. They suspect that one apartment in the building is serving as a warehouse for a "fence." But which apartment is it? One police officer suggests that the police seal the exits to the building. Then, he says, they should go through the apartments, one by one, until they find the one with the stolen goods. Another officer laughs at this suggestion. He says that this will ruin their case. Why?
- A policeman stops a car for running a red light. While talking to the driver, the officer suspects that the driver has been drinking. He tells the driver that he is going to search the car. The driver says that the car is his personal property and that the policeman has no right to search it. Who is right?

1. Privacy

In one way or another, both of these cases are about the right of privacy. Case One is about the right to keep the government from entering private homes. Case Two is about the right of citizens to protect their property against government searches.

Privacy is one of our most cherished rights. The idea that "a man's home is his castle" is basic to our system of laws. Americans believe strongly that the police cannot just barge into their homes and inspect their property.

But no right is absolute. Privacy is important. But society also needs to protect itself against crime. One way to do this is by collecting evidence. Sometimes evidence cannot be gathered without invading a citizen's privacy. Is it worth it? No one can say for sure. Every case is different. Society must always balance the right of privacy against the need for law and order. This problem of balance has been with us since colonial times. It is still with us today.

The Fourth Amendment

The right of privacy has always been important to Americans. During colonial times, the British tried to stop smuggling by American merchants. Britain issued papers called "writs of assistance." These writs allowed British officials to search a person's home or business. The British could even search the clothes the person was wearing. They could also seize any items they wished as evidence.

When the Bill of Rights was added to the Constitution, the Fourth Amendment set forth the basic right of privacy for all Americans.

The Fourth Amendment does not ban *all* searches and seizures — only ones that are "unreasonable." In other words, it does not give the right to *absolute* privacy. It limits what police can do when they make a search.

But what is an unreasonable search? The courts are constantly being asked to rule on this question. They have said that a search is unreasonable unless the police first obtain a warrant or have a very good reason for not obtaining one.

To obtain a search warrant, the police must convince a judge that there is a real need to search the person or place. This real need is known to lawyers as *probable cause*. If the judge agrees, he or she will give the police a court order that allows them to make the search. (We will look at the acceptable reasons for making a search *without* a warrant in the next section.)

Search warrants do not give the police the right to search where, when, and what they want. The Fourth Amendment says that search warrants must describe "the place to be searched, and the person or things to be seized." This means that the warrant must state where the police may make their search and exactly what they are seeking. The courts have ruled that even when the police have a warrant, a search and seizure is unreasonable if it goes beyond the reason for the search. For example, if the police search a man's home for stolen television sets, they are not allowed to take or read his personal letters.

Your Turn

1. How does the Fourth Amendment guarantee the right to privacy? Why is it said that this right is not absolute? What are some of the limits on the right of the police to search for evidence? Do you think these limits are fair? Or do they hinder the police too much?

2. The police receive an anonymous tip that Bill Green is using his house to store stolen goods. On the strength of this tip, the police ask for a search warrant to allow them to search Bill's apartment. As a judge, would you consider this tip a good enough reason to issue a search warrant? Why or why not?

3. Study the search warrant shown on the next page. Who requested it? Why was the warrant requested? Where are the searchers to look? What are they to look for? What was the position of the person who signed the warrant?

Search Warrant No. 415

STATE OF CALIFORNIA
COUNTY OF LOS ANGELES
SEARCH WARRANT

1
2
3
4   PEOPLE OF THE STATE OF CALIFORNIA to any sheriff,
5 policeman or peace officer in the County of Los Angeles:
6 PROOF by affidavit having been made before me by
7 (Name) __JOHN DOE__ that there is probable cause
8 to believe that the property described herein may be found at
9 the locations set forth herein and that it falls within those
10 grounds indicated below by "x" (s) in that it:
11 _____ was stolen or embezzled
12 __X__ was used as the means of committing a felony
13 __X__ is possessed by a person with the intent to use it as a
14   means of committing a public offense or is possessed by
15   another to whom he may have delivered it for the purpose
16   of concealing it or preventing its discovery
17   is evidence which tends to show that a felony has been
18   committed or a particular person has committed a felony;
19 you are therefore COMMANDED to SEARCH 22112 Weed Street, Los Angeles,
20 Los Angeles County, California, a frame and stucco building with
21 the numbers 22112 on the plate glass window on the south side of the
22 door, the door is plate glass and is located on the north side of the front
23 of the building, "Barber Shop" is in bold letters on the glass south of
24 the door, a rotating barber pole sign is located on the north side of the
25 door at the top of the door.
26
27 for the following property: cannabis sativa, more commonly known as
28 marijuana, and also equipment and paraphernalia used in the usage, packaging
29 and preparation of marijuana, and also articles of personal property tending
30 to establish the identity of the person or persons in control of 22112 Weed
31 Street, Los Angeles, California, consisting in part of and including, but not
32 limited to, utility company receipts, rent receipts, cancelled mail, envelopes,
33 letters and keys.
34
35
36 and to SEIZE it if found and bring it forthwith before me, or this
37 court, at the courthouse of this court.
38   Good cause having been shown by affidavit, you may do such of
39 the following as bear my initials.
40 __X__ You may serve this Warrant at any time of the day or night,
41   according to Penal Code Section 1533.
42 _____ You need not comply with Penal Code Section 1531.
43 GIVEN under my hand and dated
44 this __7th__ day of __April__ 197__8__

                                                Fred Taylor
                                                  Magistrate
                                                        Fifth
Judge of the _____ Court   Judicial District
      Superior Municipal

2.
When is a search warrant not needed?

The Fourth Amendment states that the police must get a search warrant before they can search any person or place. But U.S. courts have ruled that search warrants are not needed in some cases. The courts have said that there are times when it would be impossible for the police to stop what they are doing and get a warrant. So, the police can legally make some types of searches without warrants. In fact, most arrests and searches today occur without warrants. But even when a search without a warrant is allowed, the police still must have "probable cause." In other words, they must have a good reason to believe the search is needed. Among the situations that do *not* require search warrants are:

Consent. A person agrees to let the police conduct a search. For example, a man permits the police to search his clothing, house, or automobile.

Hot pursuit. The police are chasing a suspect and know where he or she is. For example, the police force their way into a house after they see a suspect enter it.

Emergency. The police must act to prevent damage or death. For example, the police search an apartment building after receiving a phoned warning that a bomb is set to go off there.

Stop-and-frisk. The police believe a crime has taken place in a certain area and are investigating it. For example, a police officer is checking a neighborhood where several robberies have taken place. The officer may give a "pat down" search for weapons to a hitchhiker whom he or she stops to question in the area.

Plain view. An object in plain view of passers-by may be seized without a warrant. For example, the police may seize a marijuana plant in a window box in front of a building.

Moving vehicle. The police may search an automobile without a warrant if they have good reason to believe it may contain something illegal. For example, suppose a reliable informant has told the police that a car contains illegal drugs. An officer may then stop and search the car.

Search during an arrest. An officer may search an arrested person or the area around him or her for concealed weapons, to prevent escape, or to prevent the destruction of evidence.

The borderline between situations that do and do not require a search warrant is not always clear-cut. This is particularly true of the last two situations described above. Such searches have often been challenged in the courts. In recent years, the U.S. Supreme Court has tended to broaden the area of reasonable searches.

Your Turn

In your own words, summarize the situations in which police may make a search without warrants. What do you think are the reasons for each of these exceptions?

3. The cigarette box search

The Constitution bans unreasonable search and seizure. But what is unreasonable? The following true case study concerns a college student, James Gustafson, who believed that the police had violated his right to privacy. He felt so strongly that, when he lost his case in the lower courts, he appealed all the way to the Supreme Court. In this case you will read the police report and the opinions of two Supreme Court justices who disagreed on the case.

75

Police Report (Part One)

On January 12, 1969, I, Lieutenant Paul Smith of the Eau Gallie, Florida, Police Department, was on routine patrol. I was fully uniformed, but was patrolling in an unmarked squad car. At about 2 A.M., I saw a 1953 white Cadillac with New York license plates weave across the center line three or four times. I also noticed that two of the passengers looked back and saw me in the squad car. The Cadillac then turned onto another street.

At this point, I turned on my flashing light and stopped the Cadillac. The driver of the car, James Gustafson, got out and faced me. I noticed at this time that Gustafson's eyes were bleary. Although I could not smell any odor of alcohol, I believed he could have been on drugs.

I then asked Gustafson to hand over his driver's license. He replied that he did not have it with him. He explained that he was a college student in the next town and had left his driver's license in his dormitory room. I then arrested Gustafson and took him into custody for driving without an operator's license.

I normally do not arrest local residents for such an offense, but, rather, ticket them. In this case, however, I arrested the suspect because he was not a resident of the town and was driving a car with out-of-state plates.

Your Turn

1. Why did Lieutenant Smith stop the car driven by James Gustafson? Do you think he had "probable cause" to stop the car? Why or why not?

2. What judgment did Lieutenant Smith make about Gustafson after stopping the car?

3. Why did Lieutenant Smith arrest Gustafson rather than give him a ticket? Do you think he had good reason to make the arrest? Why or why not?

Police Report (Part Two)

After placing Gustafson under arrest, I searched him. I did not feel threatened in any way by the suspect. But I always search persons I have arrested for weapons and evidence before putting them into my patrol car.

I proceeded to pat down Gustafson's clothing, outside and inside. I checked the belt, the shirt pockets, and all around the inside of his coat. In the left front coat pocket, I found a Benson & Hedges cigarette box. When I opened it, I found what I believed to be marijuana cigarettes.

Your Turn

1. On what legal basis did Lieutenant Smith search James Gustafson?
2. Was the search unreasonable in any way? Explain.

The trial

James Gustafson went to trial for having the marijuana. The first charge against him had been driving without a license. It was dropped when he produced his license.

His lawyer admitted that Gustafson was properly arrested for not having a driver's license. He also agreed that the police officer even had the right to conduct a "pat down" search for weapons. However, Gustafson's lawyer argued, the search of the cigarette box was the kind of unreasonable search banned by the Fourth Amendment. He said the officer did not have *probable cause* to search the cigarette box.

The judge at Gustafson's trial ruled that the search of the cigarette box was legal. The marijuana cigarettes were then used as evidence. Gustafson was found guilty of illegal possession of marijuana.

Gustafson appealed his case through the state courts to the Florida Supreme Court. It ruled against him. He then took his case to the U.S. Supreme Court. He argued that his Fourth Amendment rights had been violated.

Your Turn

1. On what basis did Gustafson's attorney challenge the search as unreasonable?

2. On what basis do you think the state courts allowed the search?

3. If you had been the trial judge in this case, would you have allowed the marijuana cigarettes to be admitted as evidence? Why or why not?

At the Supreme Court

Gustafson v. Florida was argued before the U.S. Supreme Court in October 1973. In December 1973, the Court announced a decision in the case. Below are the opinions of two of the Supreme Court justices in the Gustafson case. Without knowing which judge was on the majority side and which was on the minority side, read both opinions. Decide for yourself if James Gustafson's rights were violated.

Justice William Rehnquist. Justice Rehnquist said in his opinion that no one disputed the fact that James Gustafson was legally arrested for not having his driver's license with him. He also said that if the arrest was lawful, the search following the arrest must also be lawful.

Justice Rehnquist argued that the police have a right to search an arrested person for evidence. If evidence is found which is not related to the crime the person was arrested for, Rehnquist said, it still should be used against him in court.

Justice Rehnquist pointed out that Lieutenant Smith had said during the trial that Gustafson seemed drunk. After all, his car was weaving on the highway, and his eyes appeared to be "bleary." Lieutenant Smith could smell no odor of alcohol. "So," Rehnquist said, "it was reasonable for the officer to search [Gustafson] for drugs that may have been the cause of the suspected intoxication."

Justice Thurgood Marshall. Justice Marshall argued that the *full* police search of Gustafson was unreasonable. He stated that there was no reason to believe Gustafson was a dangerous person. There was also no reason to think he might have a knife or a gun in the cigarette box. "The opening of the package had no connection whatsoever with the protective purpose of the search," Marshall said.

Justice Marshall said there was not enough reason to think that Gustafson was under the

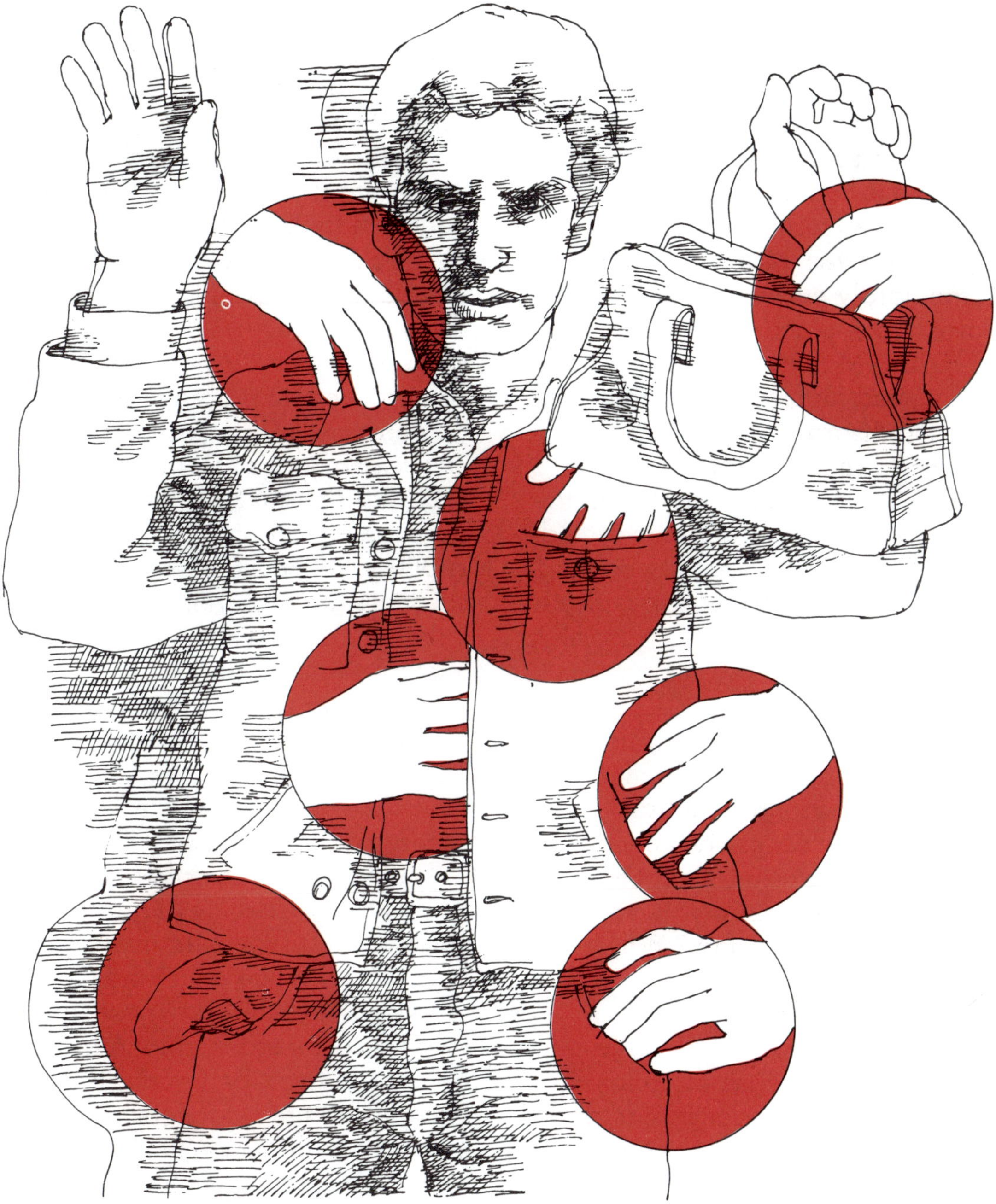

influence of drugs. Therefore there was no good reason for the full search of his clothing. Marshall noted that no sobriety test was given to the suspect. The police officer himself testified that Gustafson had no trouble getting out of his car. He did not slur his speech. As for Gustafson's "bleary" eyes, Marshall said, "that was hardly surprising since the arrest took place at 2 A.M."

Justice Marshall then said: "The only need for a search in this case was to disarm [Gustafson] to protect Officer Smith from harm while the two were together in the patrol car. The search conducted by Officer Smith went far beyond what was reasonably necessary to achieve that end."

Your Turn

1. What is the main argument of each opinion? Which argument do you think is stronger? Why?

2. The right to privacy often conflicts with society's right to investigate crime. Do you feel one right is more important? Why?

The outcome

Your teacher can tell you the decision in the case of *James Gustafson v. Florida*. It is on page 25 of the teaching guide for this book.

4.
The exclusionary rule

The Fourth Amendment protects citizens against "unreasonable searches and seizures." But it does not state what should happen if the police act illegally. This has been left to the courts.

The Supreme Court recently decided to review this question. In general, however, it has ruled that evidence taken during an illegal search cannot be used in a person's trial. This is called the *exclusionary rule*. That's because it *excludes* certain kinds of evidence from the courtroom. For example, suppose the police break into a suspect's home without a search warrant and find some stolen televison sets. Under the exclusionary rule, the sets cannot be used in court as evidence. That's because the police violated the Fourth Amendment in gathering the evidence.

The exclusionary rule does *not* prevent the arrest or trial of a suspect. It prevents the use in the court of evidence which has been obtained illegally. However, the rule sometimes *does* mean that a defendant must be freed. That's because an important piece of evidence cannot be used in the trial. As a result, some people have urged the courts to modify the exclusionary rule.

Your Turn

Why do you think the Supreme Court adopted the exclusionary rule? Do you agree with it?

Below is a case which shows the exclusionary rule in action. Discuss the case with your classmates and decide whether or not you support or oppose this rule.

The anonymous tip

On a tip from an anonymous caller, the police went to the home of Dave Gates, 18, to look for stolen eight-track tape cartridges. The officers did not have a search warrant. When they arrived, the police saw Dave run into his house. The officers ran in after him and found him in his bedroom. After a brief search, the officers found a half-dozen tapes which were later found to have been stolen. However, in court the case was dismissed. The stolen tapes could not be used as evidence since the court ruled they had been seized illegally. Without this evidence, the district attorney had no case.

• Why do you think the police officers failed to get a search warrant?

• Which of Dave's rights were violated by the police?

• Despite the fact that Dave's rights were violated, he was still caught with the stolen goods. Do you think Dave should have been tried anyway, and the tape cartridges introduced as evidence against him?

Resource person. You may wish to invite a judge or representatives from the district attorney's office, public defenders, or police officers to discuss the pros and cons of the exclusionary rule.

Chapter 7
Arrest and Your Rights

It was 12:35 A.M. when Officer Scott Harris heard the dispatcher on his two-way radio: "Attention all cars! A 211 [robbery] in progress at the Shady Glen Liquor Store, 500 South Main. Suspects armed. Proceed with caution."

Harris spun his car around and stepped down on the gas. He sped along Main for five blocks. At the Shady Glen Liquor Store he found the clerk lying on the floor with a gunshot wound. Quickly he called for an ambulance. Then he began to interview witnesses.

In another patrol car, Officers McCarty and Swenson also responded to the call. As they approached the 500 block on Main, a blue Chevrolet sped from the area. Could the two people in the car be involved with the robbery? McCarty turned on his red light and followed the blue car closely. The blue car stopped and the two police officers raced up to it, preparing to question the suspects.

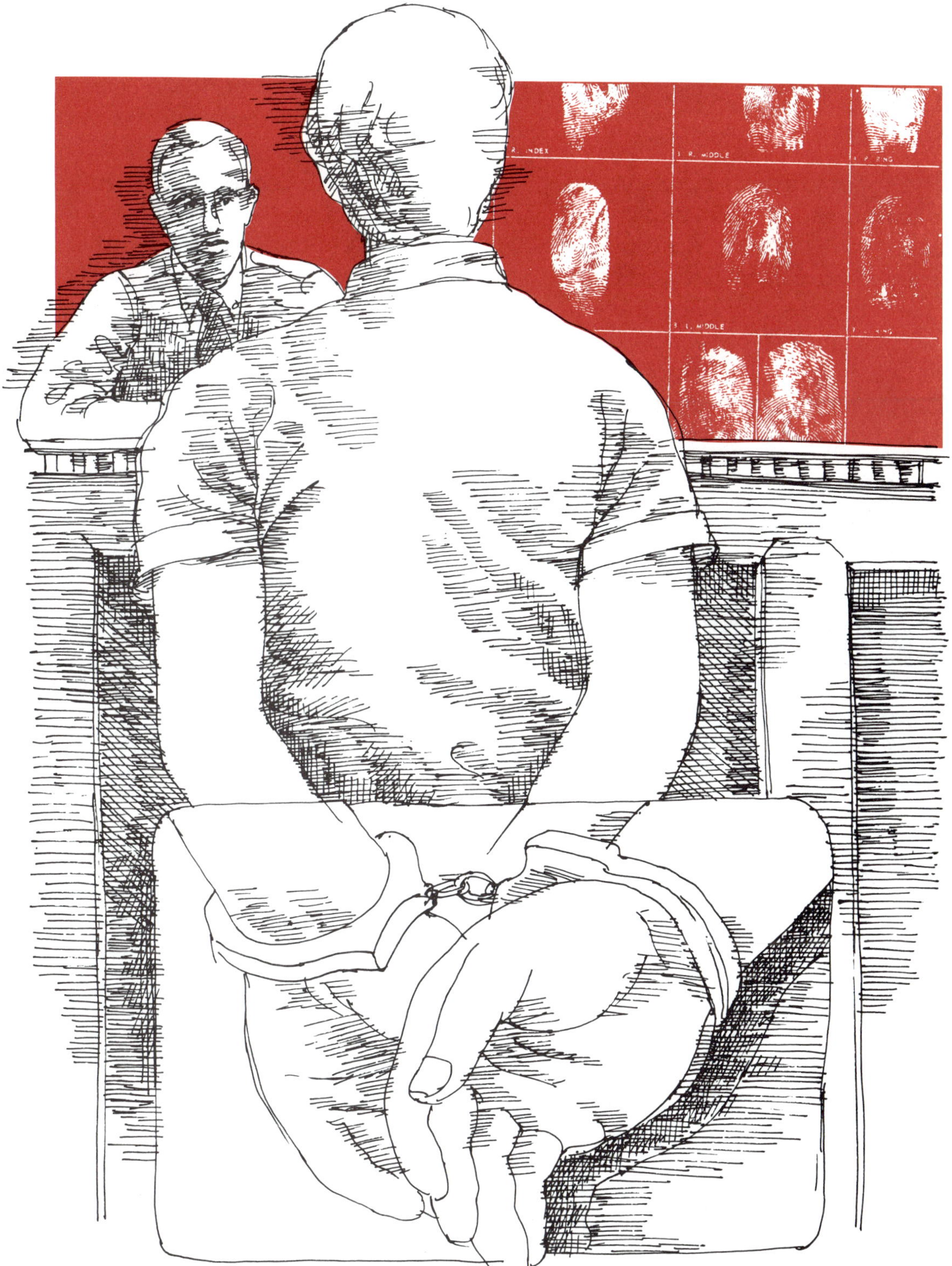
R. INDEX
R. MIDDLE
L. MIDDLE

1. Arrest

The main purpose of an arrest is to take custody of a suspect until he or she is brought to trial. An arrest means that the person taken into custody is suspected of a crime. It does *not* mean a person is guilty — or not guilty. That is for a jury to decide.

In making an arrest, a police officer must use his or her own judgment. An officer may *stop* a person if he is "reasonably suspicious" that the person is involved in a crime. For example, let's say a woman yells that her purse has been snatched. An officer sees a man running down the street one block away. The officer could *stop* the man.

But stopping a person is not an arrest. An officer may *arrest* a person if he has "probable cause" to believe the person has committed a crime. "Probable cause" is that legal phrase we used in discussing police searches (see page 71). It means that the officer must have a good reason to believe the person has committed a crime. For example, if a police officer questioning the suspect in the purse-snatching sees a bulge in the suspect's jacket as well as the strap of the purse, the officer would then have probable cause to arrest him. Probable cause is a strong *belief* that the person committed the crime. It must be based on some evidence.

In cases of minor crimes, called *misdemeanors*, a police officer must either see the crime being committed or have an arrest warrant signed by a judge before making an arrest. In cases involving more serious crimes, called *felonies*, an arrest warrant is not needed. But the officer must still have probable cause to believe the person committed the crime.

Why do you suppose an arrest warrant is not needed in cases involving serious crimes?

After an arrest, the suspect is brought to the police station and booked. *Booking* is the formal listing of a person and the crime committed. Here, again, a suspect's rights must be considered. The Sixth Amendment guarantees that the suspect will "be informed of the nature of the accusation." Booking helps to do this. After booking, the suspect is fingerprinted and photographed. The personal property of the suspect is taken and stored. A suspect is allowed to make two phone calls before being placed in a cell.

Arrest: a role-play

a. Divide the class into groups of six (three suspects and three police officers).

b. The members of each group should review the facts of the robbery situation described at the beginning of this chapter. The officers should decide what questions they will ask the suspects in the car. On the basis of the suspects' answers, the officers must decide whether to arrest the suspects. Officers should be prepared to defend their decision with evidence to support "probable cause."

Suspects should keep their own best interests in mind. They should be prepared to explain what they were doing in the neighborhood.

c. When the role-play is finished, the class should discuss the activity using the following questions:

- Was an arrest made? Why or why not?
- How were the rights of the suspects protected in this incident? The rights of society?

Resource person. You may wish to invite a law enforcement officer to visit your class and talk about his or her experiences. The officer may even want to take part in the arrest role-play.

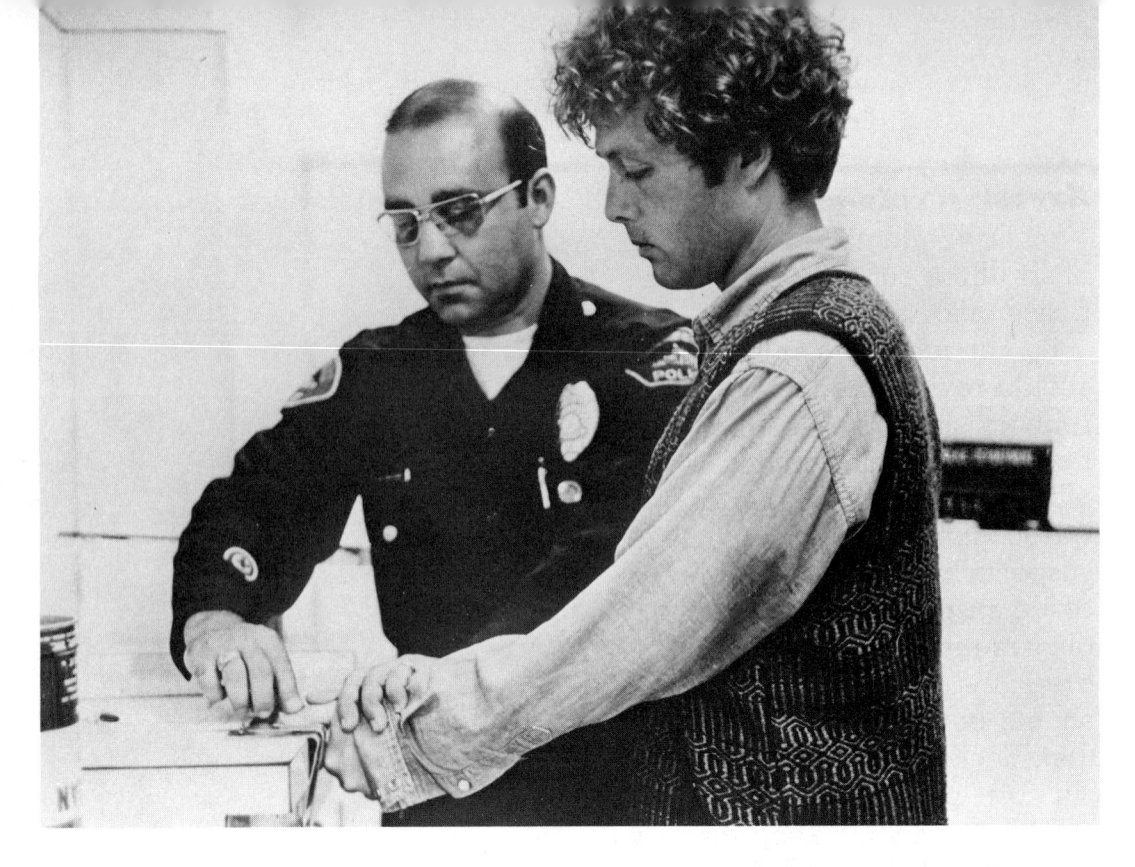

2.
Questioning suspects

From the time of an arrest until a suspect is officially charged with a crime, the police are allowed to question the suspect. Through questioning, the police hope to find out more about the crime. They also hope to learn about the suspect's part in the crime — if there is any. The police may hope the suspect will confess to committing the crime.

Anything a suspect says while being questioned may be used against him or her in court. For this reason, a confession can be a very damaging thing. At times, the police have gone too far in their wish to get a confession. So courts have developed certain rules controlling how the police may question a suspect.

Are confessions reliable?

Less than 50 years ago, the police often used force to get people to confess to crimes. Sometimes beating was done openly. But in 1936, the U.S. Supreme Court threw out a murder conviction in a case in which a suspect had been openly beaten to force a confession. The Court said that a confession based on beatings is just not believable. It cannot be accepted as evidence. As a result of this ruling, all confessions must be given freely before they can be used as evidence.

Yet just how much freedom should be given to a suspect who is being questioned? The police see it as their duty to question suspects as effectively as possible. Thus some police science schools suggest that suspects be put in an isolated room for the questioning. This room has no windows or pictures. Officers are told to appear sure that the suspect is guilty. They should play down how serious the crime is. If a person refuses to talk, he or she should be told that it looks as if the suspect has something to hide.

Sometimes the police use the "Mutt and Jeff" approach. Two officers take turns asking a suspect questions. The first officer (Mutt) comes across as tough and unfriendly. The second (Jeff) is friendly. Often after an hour of heavy questioning from Mutt, a suspect is eager to talk freely with Jeff. A confession often results.

Some officers may sometimes use deception to get a person to confess. A suspect may be told that there is some evidence linking him to the crime when actually there is none. Or, let's say more than one person is arrested for a crime.

One of the suspects may be told falsely that his friend has already confessed and has involved him.

Are these methods proper? Many people think they are. Most officers believe that some tricks are necessary in order to convict criminals. They say that not many guilty people are going to freely confess to a crime.

On the other hand, there are many people who believe that these methods are dangerous. Critics say that innocent people can get caught in a web of their own words. Thus, they may make false confessions because they do not have a lawyer's aid. Other people may become confused because they do not know their rights. Or disturbed people may panic and confess to crimes they did not commit.

Your Turn

1. What rights must be balanced against each other in deciding what methods of questioning are proper?

2. Give two examples of tricks in questioning. Do you think these are proper? Explain.

3. How would you feel if you were being questioned as a suspect in a bare, isolated room? Do you think these feelings could affect what you would say?

3. The right to counsel

Under the Sixth Amendment, a person accused of a crime has the right to be aided by a lawyer. We know that a person has a right to have a lawyer at his or her trial. But does a person have the right to counsel before trial? Say a person is being questioned by the police. Can he or she demand that a lawyer be present?

On January 31, 1960, Chicago police arrested a 22-year-old man named Danny Escobedo. The police wanted to question him about the murder of his brother-in-law. At the police station, Escobedo refused to talk. He told the officers that he would like to have advice from his lawyer.

Soon after this, Escobedo's lawyer appeared at the station house. He asked to see Danny right away. He was told to wait until the police were finished questioning the suspect.

During the questioning, Escobedo said a number of times that he wanted to talk with his lawyer. The police said no, not until the questioning was finished. Finally they were able to get Escobedo to say things that seemed to prove he had been involved in the murder. These statements were later used in court against Escobedo.

Escobedo was found guilty of murder. He then appealed his case to the U.S. Supreme Court. The legal issue in this case was whether a suspect has a right to a lawyer while he is questioned. In other words, were Escobedo's rights violated because the police would not let him see his lawyer while he was being questioned?

By a vote of 5–4 the Supreme Court decided that the Chicago police had violated Danny's rights. It said that in many cases the key time for a person accused of a crime is *not* during his trial. Instead, it is when he is questioned before his trial.

Because of the Escobedo case, an important change came about in the use of confessions. Now a suspect, who wants to, must be allowed to see his or her lawyer. If not, any confession the suspect might make to the police is not considered reliable. It makes no difference if the suspect made the confession freely. It cannot be used at the trial.

Your Turn

1. Does the Escobedo decision mean that a lawyer must always be present during questioning? What *does* it mean?

2. Do you think the "Escobedo rule" is fair to suspects? To society? Why or why not?

The Miranda decision

Danny Escobedo asked for his lawyer. But what about those people who do not realize they have the right to have a lawyer present during questioning? Or people who don't know that they need not answer police questions? Suppose they confess without knowing their rights? Can the confessions be used in court?

On March 3, 1963, an 18-year-old girl was raped near Phoenix, Arizona. Later the police arrested Ernesto Miranda for the crime. Miranda did not ask to see a lawyer. He answered the questions put to him by the police. At first, Miranda claimed he was not guilty. Later he confessed. At his trial, he was given a lawyer named by the court. His confession was used against him during the trial. As a result, he was found guilty and sentenced to 20 to 30 years in prison.

Miranda appealed his case. He said that the police should have told him that he had a right to remain silent. They should have also told him he had the right to have a lawyer present during the police questioning.

Danny Escobedo, left, with his lawyer.

In 1966 the U.S. Supreme Court ruled in favor of Miranda. The Court said Miranda's confession could not be used because he had not been told his rights. The Court said that there is tremendous pressure when the police question a person. Therefore, the police must first tell a person of his rights.

After this ruling, Miranda was given a second trial. Although his confession was not used during the trial, he was found guilty again on other evidence.

Miranda rights

The Miranda decision affected far more people than just Ernesto Miranda. For in it, the Supreme Court listed the rights the police must observe before confessions can be used as evidence. When the police arrest a person, they must follow these rules.

- Before any questioning, the police must tell a person that he has the right to remain silent. They must also tell him that anything he says may be used against him in court.

- The police must also tell the suspect of his right to a lawyer. If he cannot afford a lawyer, he must be told that the state will provide one. The suspect may have the lawyer present during the questioning.

- The suspect may give up these rights. But he must do this freely, knowing what his rights are.

- The suspect has the right to request a lawyer *at any time* after being taken into custody by the police. He can also stop answering questions at any time after his arrest.

The arguments

The Miranda and Escobedo rulings have forced changes in the way the police must deal with suspects. Thus, these rulings have caused a great deal of controversy. Many people favor the rulings, because they believe that the rulings make sure that a person's rights will be respected. These people also say that the decisions force law enforcement agencies to do their job more carefully. The argument goes that more real criminals will be found guilty. And people who are innocent will not go to jail.

On the other hand, many people oppose these rulings on the grounds that the rulings make it too hard for the police to do their work. Critics say the police cannot do their job properly and cannot question suspects in a way that will get the guilty to confess. These people say that the effect of these decisions is to "coddle" criminals.

Miranda limited

In recent years, new rulings by the Supreme Court have given more detail as to what the police can and cannot do.

One recent Court ruling was that the police must honor *all* requests from suspects for a lawyer. The police must also stop questioning whenever a suspect asks for a lawyer, or simply asks them to stop questioning. They may resume questioning later only at the suspect's request. If a suspect refuses to talk to the police, this fact may not be used against him or her in court.

New Court decisions have also placed some limits on suspects' rights. For example, say a witness is found through "leads" in a suspect's statements to the police. This witness may testify against the suspect in court. He or she may do this even though the lead was gained illegally.

Your Turn

1. Go back to the case of the Memphis Five (pages 11–33). What was the first thing that Officer Davis said to John and Laurie during their arrest? What is the connection between this and the Miranda case?

2. How was the Miranda case like the Escobedo case? How was it different?

3. Do you think the Miranda decision is fair to suspects? To society? Why or why not?

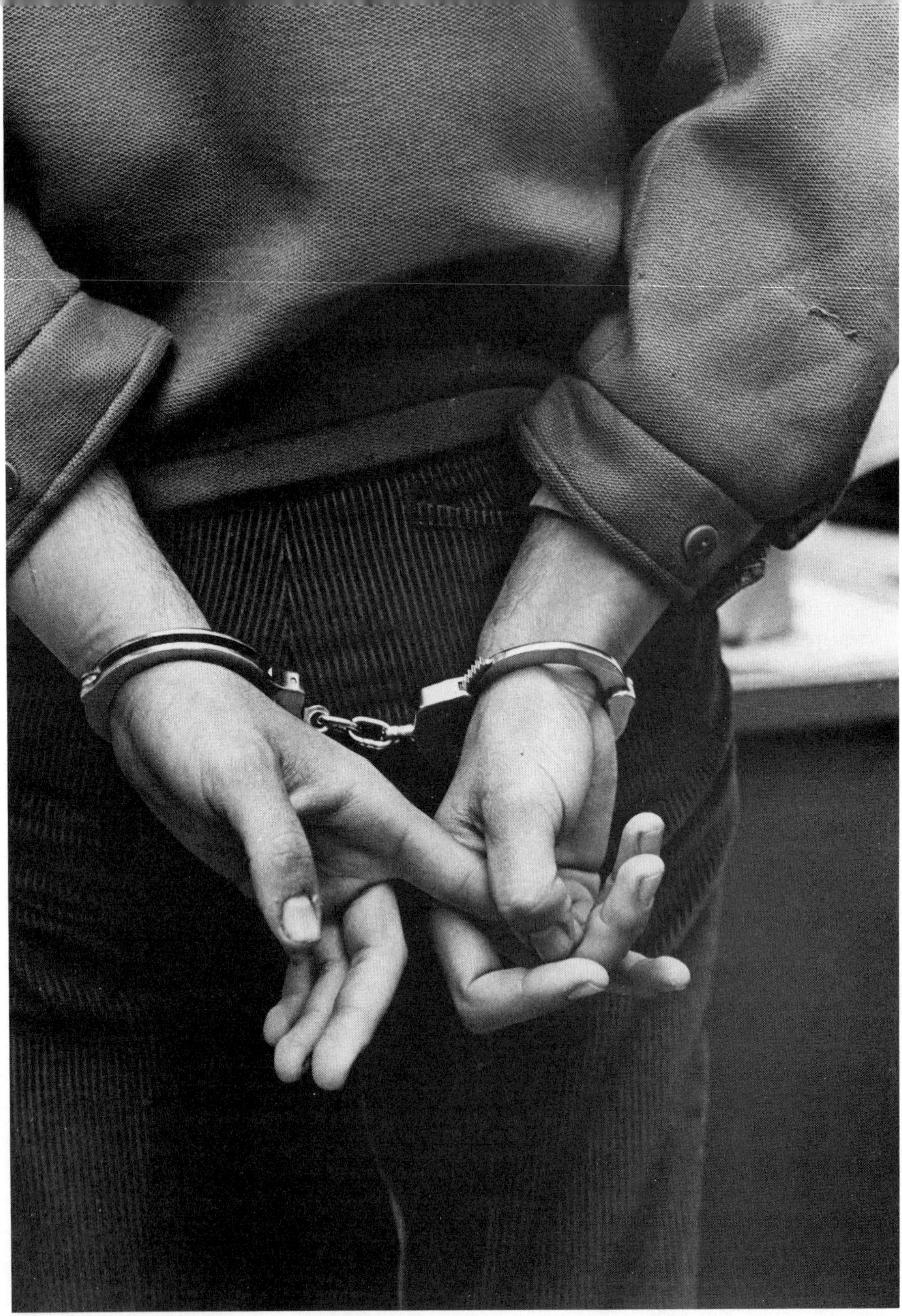

4. Jimmy Tyson and the big fire

Is it important for a suspect to have a lawyer with him during police questioning? Sometimes it is and sometimes it isn't.

A person may be frightened or confused when questioned in a police station. Some people may say foolish things. And these foolish things can be used against them in court. In cases such as these, the law must take into account human weakness.

For example, in the following case, a young man confessed to setting a fire that killed 25 people. However, questions arose over whether or not to believe his confession. The names of the suspect and the officers who questioned him have been changed to protect them, but the case is true.

Jimmy Tyson's story

On the morning of June 1, 1975, Jimmy Tyson arrived in Denver on a bus. The 125-pound, six-foot youth had just turned 18. He had left home in Dallas after an argument with his mother. She was upset with him because he had recently been sent to a school for delinquents for setting a series of small fires.

When he got off the bus in Denver, Jimmy had five dollars in cash and two Dallas bus tokens. Not knowing where to go, Jimmy walked for a long time.

That night an old apartment building, the Surrey, burned down. Twenty-five people were killed in the fire. Fire officials suspected arson. The Surrey was not far from the bus station.

Early the next morning, Jimmy Tyson was awakened on a bench by two police officers. He was 14 miles from the Surrey. The two policemen thought at first that Jimmy might be a runaway. He looked about 16. When the officers began to ask him questions, Jimmy became nervous. His speech was choked and he kept wiping his sweaty hands on his pants. He told the officers that he had arrived in Denver the morning before. Jimmy said that he had walked and taken a bus to where he was now. The police asked if he had been in trouble before. Jimmy answered that he had recently been released from a training school for setting fires. That was enough for the police officers to arrest Jimmy.

The first questioning

Soon after Jimmy was brought into

the police station, the morning newspaper arrived. Jimmy was shown a picture of the burning building.

"Is this place familiar to you?" one of the officers asked.

Jimmy stared at the picture. He looked at the headlines, TWENTY-FIVE DEAD, 40 INJURED IN APARTMENT BLAZE. Jimmy became very nervous. He started to mutter to himself, "Dead, death, dead."

"Were you at this apartment house last night?" the officer asked.

"No, no. I don't know anything about it," Jimmy said.

Later a policeman lit a cigarette next to Jimmy. Jimmy jerked in his seat, turned toward the flame, and stared at it. He almost seemed hypnotized.

The second questioning

Jimmy was next turned over to Officer Russell. Jimmy agreed to talk to Russell without a lawyer present. Jimmy described his troubled life. He said that he had dropped out of school after the ninth grade. At age 16, he had been arrested for setting trash fires. Because of this, he had spent a year in the training school.

Officer Russell told Jimmy that some witnesses had seen a person who looked like him at the Surrey shortly before the big fire broke out. Jimmy looked puzzled. In fact, this was not true.

Jimmy then agreed to take a lie-detector test. The two-hour test began with an officer asking Jimmy over and over again if he had set any fires in Denver. Jimmy was not certain.

The lie-detector test gave no clear answer as to whether Jimmy had set the fire.

The confession

After taking the test, Jimmy was turned over once again to Officer Russell. At this point, Jimmy had not slept for 36 hours.

"Hi, Jimmy," said Russell. "Kind of tired, huh?" Russell asked whether Jimmy had been treated for mental illness. Was he better now? Russell also asked whether Jimmy had seen a mattress at the Surrey.

"Did you light a match on a couch or was it a mattress?" asked Russell.

"I can't remember," answered Jimmy.

"OK, but you remember that you set the fire because you wanted to kill your mother, right?" said Russell.

"Yes, sir," replied Jimmy.

Jimmy Tyson was booked on 25 counts of murder and one count of arson.

Your Turn

1. As described above, does the questioning of Jimmy Tyson follow the Escobedo rule? Does it follow the Miranda rule? Why or why not?

2. What tactics did the police use to try to make Jimmy confess? Do you think these were justified? Why or why not?

3. Do you think it is possible for an innocent person to confess to a serious crime?

The outcome

Your teacher can tell you what happened to Jimmy Tyson. It is on page 27 of the teaching guide for this book.

Chapter 8
Police Power

It happened without warning.

The police radio said the robbery suspect might be armed, and the two officers knew they should take no chances. So, when they spotted the man, they braked their patrol car, drew their revolvers, and approached with caution.

But they never guessed the suspect had a partner. Shots rang out. The officers' failure to watch the door behind them cost them their lives — or would have, if the shots had not been blanks, and if it all had not been a training exercise at the firearms training school of the New York City police.

"What you think you see and what you really have is not always the same," the instructor booms at the 75 watching police officers as their two colleagues return sheepishly to the viewing stand.

"Remember, the harmless-looking fellow on the corner could have a gun, and the suspicious-looking guy you stopped to question could be an honest man on his way home from work."

— Excerpted by permission from The Christian Science Monitor, 1975. The Christian Science Publishing Society. All rights reserved.

Department of Police
This is to certify that
JOHN SMITH
Height
5'9"
Weight
155 lbs.
Brown
Brown
Chief of Police
K5
D2
K4
D3
K3
D5

Police work can be dangerous. A New York City plainclothes officer, shot in the course of an investigation, dies in the arms of another policeman.

1. The danger of police work

Police work *is* dangerous. Split-second decisions police officers may be forced to make could cost them their lives. Or they could result in a civilian being killed for no good reason. A police officer must know when to shoot — and when *not* to shoot. Thus, good judgment is a matter of life and death for both civilian and officer.

Few groups in the U.S. are in greater danger of violent attack than police officers. For example, in the period between 1972 and 1981, a total of 1,109 police officers were killed in the line of duty. Most police deaths occurred during arrests.

Because police officers are in danger, they may react too quickly. Sometimes they make mistakes and shoot innocent citizens, or kill a suspect instead of capturing him or her. Some people say that although these shootings are bad, a certain number are bound to happen. Such incidents are unavoidable, they say, as long as the police themselves face continual danger.

Others disagree. They charge that the police are often too fast to use their guns. They also say that many police are not properly trained, or look on minority-group members as enemies.

Meanwhile, many police departments have developed "firearms policies." These policies are designed to give police officers detailed guidance on when and where to use their guns.

Your Turn

1. Describe the basic conflict over the police use of firearms.

2. You are a police officer trying to stop a riot. Looters are breaking into stores and carrying off goods. You spot one looter rushing out of a jewelry store with a handful of watches. You yell at him to stop and fire a few warning shots with your handgun. The looter looks over his shoulder at you, but continues running. You know you will not be able to catch him, but he is still within firing range. What do you do? Shoot to kill? Shoot to wound, knowing that you are more likely to miss? Let the looter escape? Other? Explain.

2. Dealing with the police

Suppose you're walking along minding your own business and a police officer stops and questions you. What should you do? When you're driving at night and an officer stops you, what is the best way to behave? What rights do police officers have? What rights do you have if the police question you or give you instructions?

Knowing what to do when you are dealing with the police may help you feel more secure. It certainly can help you to do what is best for you.

Peer teaching. This section is designed for peer teaching. If you wish to peer teach the section, first make arrangements with your teacher. You might also ask a lawyer to come into your class and help you.

What right do juveniles have? Even though juveniles are handled differently than adults in the justice system, you have *most* of the same rights. For example, you have the right of freedom of speech, the right to remain silent, and the right to have a lawyer present after you have been arrested. As a minor, you do *not* have the right to bail. Nor do you have the right to a jury trial.

This does not mean that young people have fewer rights than adults. A juvenile hearing is not supposed to find guilt. Rather, it is supposed to do what is best for each young person.

What rights do police officers have? A law enforcement officer has rights and duties. He or she has the *duty* to protect the community, to see to it that the laws are obeyed, and to catch criminals. The police officer has a right to perform this duty. This is his or her job. In addition, the officer has the duty to serve the public. That includes you. You, in turn, have a duty as a citizen to give reasonable help to a police officer when he or she requests it.

Do you have to answer the police officer's questions when he or she stops you? The courts have ruled that when a police officer has a good reason to stop you, generally you should identify yourself and explain what you are doing in the area (see page 84). However, if the officer asks you questions which seem to be connecting you to some crime, you have the right to stop talking.

Can the police stop and frisk you on the street? Yes, if the officer has probable cause to believe that you have committed a crime (or are about to) and might be armed.

For example, if a crime had just been reported in a neighborhood and you look like the suspect, the officer might have the right to stop and frisk you. Remember, the police do *not* have to be certain you are guilty. They only have to have some evidence that you might be involved in a crime.

What is the best thing to do when you are stopped on the street by the police? Cooperate. Do this even if you *know* you are innocent of any wrongdoing. Give any basic information the police want (name, address, where you are going, etc.). In most cases you will then be allowed to move on.

Do *nothing* to make an officer angry. If you refuse to answer questions connecting you to some crime, do so politely. Arguing or talking back can never help you.

What is the best thing to do when you are stopped in a car? Stop the car and sit tight. Do not make any sudden movements. If you are stopped at night, a good practice is to turn on your dome light and place your hands on the steering wheel. This should put the officer at ease. You will probably be asked for your driver's license and car registration. You *must* turn over these documents to the officer.

Then follow the suggestions in the answer to the question immediately above.

What if the police come to your house and want to enter it? You do not have to let the police into your house unless they have a search warrant. (See page 72.) If you allow the police to come into your house *without* a search warrant, you can set limits on what they may do. For example, you can tell them they may wait for a suspect to return, or they may look in each room but not search inside drawers or cases.

What if the police have a search warrant? Ask to see it. Make sure it contains the correct street address of your home. Look to see what items are listed on the warrant to be searched for in your home. The police are supposed to search only for these items.

What should you do if you believe that the police have violated your rights? For example, suppose they overstep the limits of a search? This is a very difficult situation for you to handle. You will probably be scared, angry, or both. Despite a desire to argue or fight back, the best thing is to be as cool as possible and remain silent. *At this point,* there is no way you can win. However, there are several things you *can* do:

a. Try to memorize the badge number or name plates of the officer(s). Be sure you can identify the officer(s).

b. Look around for persons you know who could be witnesses for you later on. Even persons you do not know might be helpful, so try to remember what they look like.

c. Go to the police station nearest you. (If you are a minor, have one of your parents go with you.) Tell the desk officer you wish to make a complaint. The desk officer should either take down the information you give, or should turn you over to a supervising officer who will do this.

If the result of the police investigation still does not satisfy you, there are further steps that can be taken. For example, you can appeal to the police commission, or ask for help from a local government office (such as the mayor's office, your city council person, your county supervisor, your state assembly person or senator). Or your parents may wish to consult an attorney.

Your Turn

What are the rights of the police to stop and question you? What are your rights when stopped and questioned?

3. Police test

John, George, and Adrienne stood at the bulletin board outside the employment office. Each read the recruiting notice for police officers. All three knew that police work can be hard. At times, it is dangerous. Not everyone is suited to such work. For this reason, people training to be police officers must take a series of tests which are designed to show if they have the right attitude, skills, and strength to do the job.

All three read the notice below:

As they read the requirements, their expressions changed. John smiled. He turned, entered the office, and asked for an application. George and Adrienne shook their heads and walked slowly out of the building. Adrienne was 19, too young to qualify. George had been convicted of auto theft three years ago.

Peer Teaching. This section is designed for peer teaching. If you wish to peer teach the section, first make arrangements with your teacher. You may also wish to invite a police officer to speak on the qualities that make a good officer.

WANTED: RECRUITS FOR CITY POLICE DEPARTMENT

Education: High school graduate or equivalent. Two or more years of college preferred. 12 units in police science very helpful.

Age: Not less than 20 years, or more than 30 years, at time of filing application

License: A valid driver's license.

Height: No restrictions.

Weight: No specific restrictions.

Character: Should not be convicted of a felony. Those convicted of misdemeanors will be subject to a review.

Your Turn

1. Why do you think there are educational standards for law enforcement officers? What people would be eliminated under such standards? Could people who don't have that education still be good police officers?
2. Why do you think there are age standards? What people would most likely be eliminated under such standards? Could members of the age groups eliminated still be good police officers?
3. Why do you think there are height and weight standards? What people would most likely be eliminated under such standards? Could members of the groups eliminated still be good police officers?
4. Do you think standards such as those listed on page 103 might affect the way laws are enforced? Explain your answer.

John's test

Because he met the requirements, John was allowed to take the test for potential police officers. The test included questions on English, arithmetic, verbal comprehension, and memory. There was also a "what-would-you-do" section. For example:

1. Which of the following is the most important for a detective to know when he is gathering evidence about a crime? (a) How to classify the fingerprints of the suspect. (b) The penalty for the particular crime that is involved. (c) What kinds of evidence are admissible in court. (d) What the reputation of the suspect is for honesty and truth. (e) What other crimes the suspect has been accused of.

2. You are sent as a police officer to discuss a minor complaint with a person who seems angry and hostile toward you. From the standpoint of good community relations, what should you do? (a) Show interest in the person's point of view. (b) Work the problem out with the person on a rational basis. (c) Record the complaint and leave. (d) Impress the person with your official capacity.

How would you answer these questions?

John passed this test and a few weeks later was interviewed and given some physical tests. At the interviews, a group of people who had had experience in police work asked John questions about his background, attitudes, reasons for wanting to do police work, and what he thought he would do in certain kinds of situations he was likely to encounter. Then John was interviewed by a psychologist. During this interview, John took tests designed to tell things about his personality. His answers would help show whether or not he might be a good police officer.

John passed all these tests. Then he filled out papers for a background check. Finally, he was accepted for police training for 16 weeks at the police academy.

Your Turn

What do you think was the purpose of each section of the test that John took? Are there any further tests you think would have been useful?

Simulation

To give you some experience with the way police officers are hired, members of the class should divide into groups of four. Your task will be to decide whether or not to hire either of two candidates for the position of police officer. (You will find reports on the two candidates on the following pages.) You should discuss the reports on each candidate and make a decision on whether to hire him and/or her. Be prepared to explain your reasons for your decision.

Candidate Report One

Name: *William John Garfield* (Male, age 22).

I. *Personal Information*
(A) 5'10." (B) 180 lbs. (C) Excellent health and vision. (D) Satisfactory appearance. (E) High school graduate (B average). (F) *Legal Record:* Arrested once for joyriding (age 14); charges dropped for lack of evidence. (G) Four-year resident of this city. (H) Valid driver's license. (I) Satisfactory high school citizenship record.

II. *Physical Test:* Passed.

III. *Psychiatrist's Report*
Candidate seems able to handle dangerous situations and would be able to use force against others if necessary. Test results show that candidate does not really understand what makes people do things. He tends to judge situations by rigid standards. Candidate has great respect for authority and a willingness to follow orders. Candidate has some hostile feelings toward his father.

IV. *Interview*
A pleasant person with officerlike bearing. He appears to be easy-going and friendly. He enjoys several hobbies including biking, camping, and hunting.

V. *Candidate's Statement*
"I would like to be a police officer because I feel respect for the law is very important and I want to help maintain the law. I would enjoy police work because it offers a lot of work tasks and because it is out-of-doors. Also, it involves helping people and sometimes it's exciting. I feel I would be a good police officer because I like to work hard and I like people and I am not afraid of dangerous situations."

Candidate Report Two

Name: *Juanita Maria Marquez* (Female, age 22).

I. *Personal Information*
(A) 5'6." (B) 130 lbs. (C) Excellent health and vision. (D) Satisfactory appearance. (E) Two years college (A average). (F) *Legal Record:* none. (G) 10-year resident of this city. (H) Valid driver's license. (I) Satisfactory high school citizenship record.

II. *Physical Tests:* Passed.

III. *Psychiatrist's Report*
Candidate is very stable and shows ability to understand others. Candidate is unsure of herself in situations involving conflict between people from different ethnic groups. She shows great respect for authority and is very religious. Candidate shows great affection for her family and enjoys people.

IV. *Interview*
Lively and friendly. Enjoys sports and is skilled in gymnastics and karate.

V. *Candidate's Statement*
"In high school I was a member of the student council. We had to face many problems at our school, including gang wars. Since that time, I have wanted to go into police work especially with juveniles and try to help solve these problems."

Your Turn

1. Tally the results for the class as a whole. What were the major reasons for or against selecting each candidate?

2. In your opinion, was the selection process fair and effective? Based on your experience with this exercise, what are the most important things that should be considered in selecting police officers?

Resource person. If you are interested in a career in law enforcement, you might invite people who work in law enforcement to visit the class. Or you could make an appointment to visit them to discuss their work.

Toward a Better System of Justice

Improving law enforcement

Over the past few weeks, your class has studied the role of police through reading, discussions, and activities.

As a result of your study, what changes or improvements in police practices do you think would make the police more just and effective in your community? In what ways do you think the police are now doing a good job in your community?

State your ideas as clearly as possible. Be specific. What would you keep? What would you change? How? You may also want to propose *new* programs or ideas. Explain why you feel your ideas would improve police work in your community.

The Badge: a Bibliography

Famous Supreme Court Cases
by Andrew David, Lerner Publications, 1980.
Includes several cases involving the rights of the accused.

The Making of a Woman Cop
by Mary Ellen Albrecht, William Morrow, 1976.
The personal experiences of a policewoman in Washington, D.C.

1984
by George Orwell, Signet, 1971.
The classic novel about a future society in which all aspects of life are controlled by "the Party." What happens when one man decides to rebel against the system? This book makes a strong statement about the importance of our right to privacy.

Police! A Precinct at Work
by Sara Ann Friedman and David Jacobs, Harcourt Brace Jovanovich, 1975.
The authors spent a year in a New York City precinct house. Here are some of the varied incidents they saw.

Youth, the Police, and Society
from the Bill of Rights Newsletter, *Constitutional Rights Foundation, 1971.*
Cartoons, surveys, Supreme Court rulings, book reviews, and interviews — all focused on the role of the police in dealing with young people.

PART 3
THE GAVEL

The Role of the Courts

Chapter 9
The Right to a Fair Trial

The purpose of a trial is to find the truth. But truth is a funny thing. It means different things at different times to different people. The ideas we hold about trials today — and how to find the truth — began to develop more than a thousand years ago in England. At that time, lawyers were unknown. Defendants had few, if any, rights. A juror could also be a witness. And people believed that God alone could judge a person's guilt or innocence. You may well wonder how today's trial system could have developed from such a start. This chapter will show you how your right to a fair trial developed. It will also describe what happens in the period before a case comes to trial.

1.
Trials:
by ordeal — by jury

All societies have laws. All societies also have ways of judging and punishing people who break the laws. One method for doing this is to hold a trial.

Today's ideas about trials developed in England in the Middle Ages. That was a time of deep religious feeling. People believed that only God knew the truth. Thus, only God could judge an accused person. People thought God would help someone on trial who was innocent.

Several kinds of trials were based on this belief. One kind of trial was called *trial by ordeal*. The idea was that God would save an innocent person with a miracle. Thus, a person accused of a crime might be forced to put his or her arm into a kettle of boiling water. Naturally, the arm would be terribly burned. If these burns healed in three days — a miracle — the defendant was innocent. Defendants sometimes carried red-hot irons with their bare hands or walked through hot coals in their bare feet. Not many defendants were saved by any miracles.

People also believed that God would help the innocent person in battle. In a *trial by combat*, accused persons could prove their innocence or defend their rights through battle. But that didn't mean that the accused themselves had to go to battle. Warriors could be hired to fight for them.

By the 12th century, many people in Europe were complaining that trial by ordeal was unfair. New rules began to grow. Courts began to demand proof before convicting a person. They demanded that witnesses to a crime testify. In some countries, the verdict in a case was made by a group of nobles or merchants. It was believed that these men would be more qualified to decide the truth in a case. This was the beginning of our modern-day jury system.

Today jurors are chosen from citizens who are called for jury duty. When we say that an accused person is entitled to a trial before his or her peers, we mean those citizens who form the jury and hear evidence in a public trial. They must decide whether a defendant is guilty or not guilty. These juries are sometimes called *petit* (little) *juries* to distinguish them from *grand* (large) *juries*. A grand jury is usually made up of respected citizens in the

Medieval trials are pictured in these prints. Two of them show trials by ordeal.

community. Its job is to hear evidence presented — in secret — by the district attorney. After hearing the evidence, the grand jury decides whether or not to accuse someone of committing a crime.

Legal battles are no longer fought by warriors using weapons. They are fought by lawyers using words. In modern courtrooms, lawyers for each side present their case to the jury. They also try to show the flaws in the other side's case. This court contest is known as the *adversary system*. It is based on the idea that when both sides in a case present their evidence, a jury will be able to find the truth of the matter.

Due process

What is a fair trial? When we ask this question, we are really asking two other questions:

1. Is the *law itself* fair to the person accused?

2. Are the *methods* fair for deciding whether an accused person is guilty or innocent?

Due process of law means those rights of accused persons which assure that both laws and trial procedures are fair. One right is to be fully informed of the proceeding against him or her. A second right is that of a public hearing (trial). During that trial, the accused person has the right to cross-examine (question and challenge) the accusers.

Due process also means that laws themselves must be fair. They must apply equally to all the people affected by them. In other words, everyone is entitled to the *equal protection of the law*. For example, a law saying that only white people can sit in the front seats of buses and that black people must sit in the back seats of buses is not a fair law because it does not apply equally to all citizens who ride buses. It deprives black people of the equal protection of the law.

Citizens who are accused of a crime are also entitled to have an attorney to defend them. But many accused persons cannot afford to hire an attorney. For them, the courts provide *public defenders*. These attorneys are hired by the courts to serve at no cost to the accused.

2. Bail or jail?

Usually an arrested person can get out of jail if he or she pays an amount of money to the court. This money is called *bail*. It assures that the accused person will return for trial.

Few people have the money on hand to post bail. Rather, they get the money from a bail bondsperson. For a fee of five to 10 percent of the bail, the bondsperson agrees to pay the total amount of the bail to the court if the defendant does not return for trial. If the accused person does *not* return for the trial, the court keeps the money. If the accused person does return, the court refunds the money.

Resource person. You may invite a lawyer and a bondsperson to visit the class. Remember, there are two sides to the bail story. Be sure to invite people on both sides.

Is bail fair?

The police in Central City were cracking down on drug dealers. During "Operation Bust," two men were arrested just as they were completing a sale of cocaine. Albert Morrison, an unemployed laborer, bought the drugs with the money he got for a stolen television set. Victor Lind, a wealthy dealer, sold him the cocaine which he had smuggled into the country.

Lind's bail was set at $10,000; Morrison's, at $3,500. Victor Lind was able to post bail by paying a bail bondsman $1,000. He went home until his next court appearance. Unfortunately, Albert Morrison had no money. He could not post bail or pay a bail bondsman. He had to remain in jail until his trial. Because the court's trial schedule was very crowded, Albert Morrison stayed in jail for seven months before he came to trial.

Your Turn

1. What is bail? What is its purpose?

2. In the case of Lind and Morrison, which man do you think was accused of the more serious crime? How well did the bail process work in this case?

Pretrial release

The criticisms of bail have led some areas to try other programs. One of these programs is called O.R. This stands for "own recognizance." It means that some specially selected defendants can be released without bail before trial. The judge makes this decision. He or she will consider the seriousness of the crime, whether the defendant has a job, and whether the defendant has other ties with the community.

A defendant released on O.R. gets help in staying within the law. Two days before any scheduled court appearance, the defendant is contacted by telephone. He or she is reminded of the date and time of appearance, and is encouraged to be in court for the appointment.

So far, many O.R. programs have been successful. Such programs have also reduced government costs for jail and family support. The key is to make sure that the person released without bail will show up for trial and will keep out of trouble. Sometimes defendants have not been properly screened. They have committed violent crimes while out on O.R. or on a very small bail.

3. Plea bargaining

Most Americans believe that an accused person always goes to trial. However, very few people who are arrested ever come to trial. One reason for this is that courts are too crowded to bring everyone to trial. The fictional case below shows another way of handling a case in which a person is accused of committing a crime.

Paul's case

Paul Kerbel sat in his cell in county jail, thinking about his problem. Two weeks ago he had been arrested for armed robbery. He tried to remember how it had happened.

He and a friend, Mike Collins, had gone to a liquor store late one evening. Mike had said the owner of the store owed him money for some debts. Although Paul didn't know it, Mike had a gun. At the liquor store, Mike and the owner got into an argument about the money. Mike pointed the gun at the owner and told him to hand the money to Paul. Paul took the money, and the two young men fled. Later that evening, both were arrested.

Paul had not intended to take part in a robbery. Now he was in real trouble. Because the court schedule was very crowded, his trial would not be held for six months. Paul could not post bail, so he would have to stay in jail.

As Paul sat thinking in his cell, his public defender stopped by for a visit. He told Paul that he could arrange a plea bargain if Paul would agree. Paul did not know what to say. He had heard of plea bargaining. But he really didn't know just what it meant.

The bargain

The public defender explained that a plea bargain is an agreement between the defense and prosecuting attorneys. It must be approved by the judge. In a plea bargain, the defendant agrees to plead guilty to a less serious crime than the one charged. There is no trial. In this way, a case can be finished quickly. Usually, a defendant who accepts a plea bargain receives a lighter sentence than if he or she had been found guilty of the more serious charge.

"I think if you would agree to plead guilty to attempted robbery, the district attorney would accept the plea," the public defender told Paul.

"But I wasn't attempting to rob anyone," Paul protested. "It was all a mistake."

"The evidence is against you, Paul," the public defender reminded him. "If you go to trial, you could be convicted on a more serious charge. And the judge would probably not be as lenient with you."

"I've never been in any trouble before," Paul said. "If I plead guilty," he went on, "I would have a criminal record, wouldn't I?"

"That's right," his attorney said, "but you would probably get a light sentence. We could ask for probation. Think about it, Paul. No plea bargain will be made unless you agree."

Paul didn't know what to do. He didn't want a criminal record. Yet he didn't want to stay in jail until his trial. And if he were found guilty of armed robbery, he could spend years in jail.

To plea bargain — or not

Plea bargaining is controversial. Defenders say that it is a good way of getting a person to talk about others who may be involved in a crime. Plea bargains also save time and the costly process of investigating a case fully for trial. Without it, the courts would be even more jammed with people waiting for trial.

On the other hand, critics charge that plea bargains may allow dangerous people to receive light sentences. In addition, lawyers can abuse plea bargaining by threatening defendants with longer sentences if they refuse to plead guilty. In these ways, plea bargains may deprive some defendants of their rights to due process.

Resource person. You may wish to invite a representative from the public defender's and/or district attorney's office to visit your class and discuss the use of plea bargaining.

Your Turn

1. What is plea bargaining? What are its advantages? Its disadvantages?
2. Consider Paul Kerbel's case. Do you think Paul should accept the plea bargain he has been offered? Why or why not?
3. In general, do you think plea bargaining is fair to accused persons? To society?

Field Activity

You may find it interesting to visit a court in your area. You will need your teacher's help to arrange with a court official for the visit. Also try to arrange to meet a judge in his or her chambers. You will need to arrange transportation for the visit. But the effort will be worthwhile.

Here are some things to keep in mind while on your visit:

1. What is the mood of the court? Is the courthouse crowded and noisy? Or is it calm and businesslike?
2. Are many people waiting in the halls for their cases to be called?
3. What is the nature of the case you see? What were the prosecutor, defense attorney, judges, witnesses, defendants, and jurors all doing during the trial?
4. Describe the questioning of one witness in the trial.
5. What was your impression of the trial? How did it differ from what you expected before the visit?

Chapter 10
Lawyers and Law

Different people want to become lawyers for many different reasons. If you asked students at a law school why they wanted to be lawyers, you might hear answers such as these: "I like to examine issues from different sides. I enjoy arguing for or against a position." "I want to make a lot of money." "I want to work for social change." "I wanted to be a musician, but I couldn't make a living." "A law degree will give me lots of career choices."

Lawyers represent people in legal actions. All lawyers must have special training in order to do their job. They must also follow certain standards of conduct. In this chapter, you will learn more about the work of lawyers and careers in law.

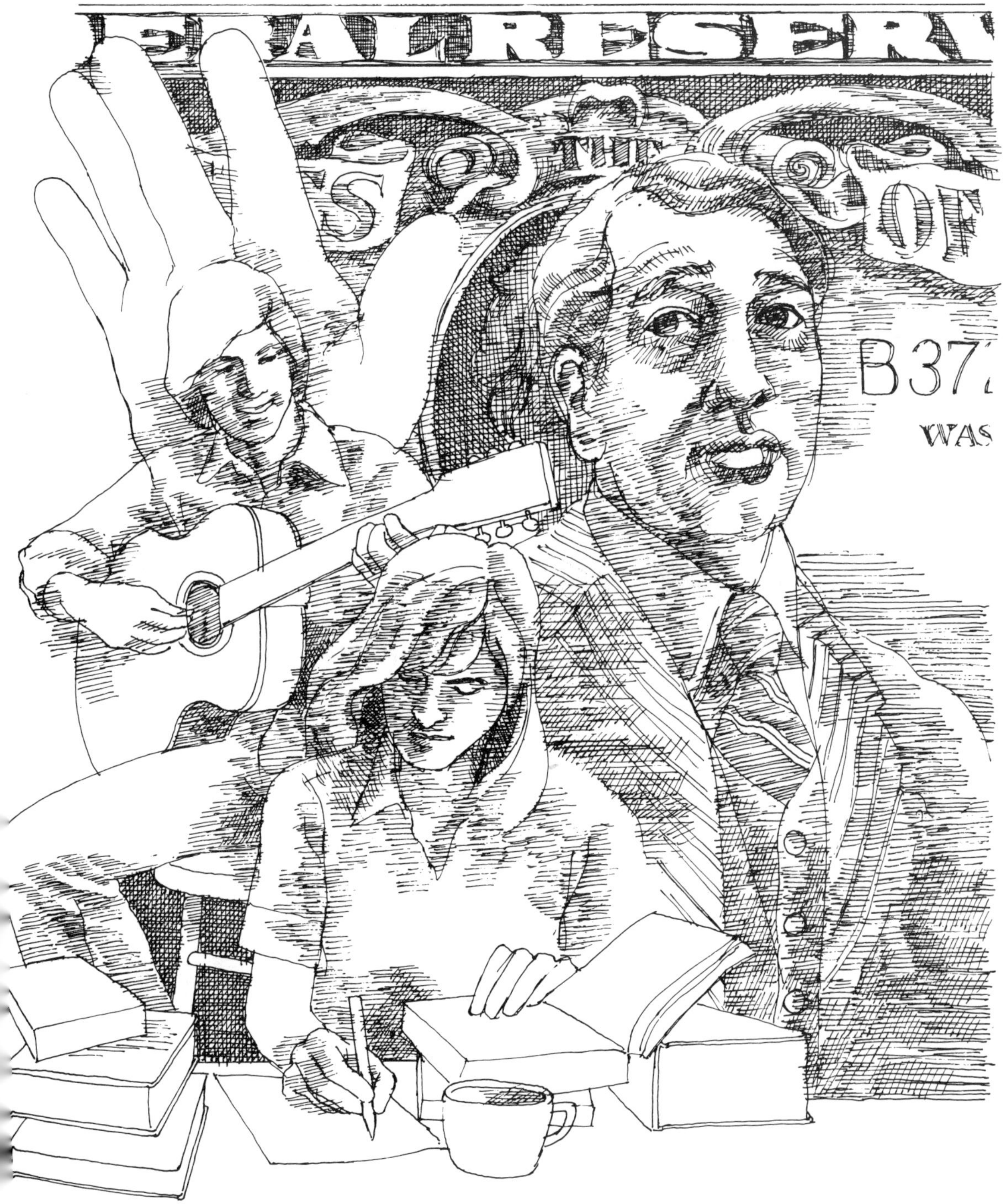
OF
B37
WAS

1. The district attorney

Each year in the U.S. several million people are arrested for felonies. Not all of these people are brought to trial because many cases are dropped before they come to trial. If a case is dropped, it is usually because the district attorney believes there is not enough evidence to convict. The district attorney is the state's prosecuting lawyer. Usually he or she decides whether to prosecute or drop a case.

In making a decision to prosecute, the district attorney considers many things. The most important questions he or she must answer are:

- Is there enough evidence to show that the crime has been committed?
- Is there enough evidence to show that the accused person committed the crime?
- Was the evidence obtained legally?

The district attorney knows there will be little or no chance of obtaining a conviction in court unless the answer to all three questions is yes. So if the answer to any one of them is no, he or she will almost certainly decide not to prosecute.

The D.A. game

In the role-play which follows, each member of the class will play the role of a district attorney. As D.A., you must decide whether or not to prosecute the three cases described on the following pages.

Divide the members of the class into six groups. Each group will act as a team of D.A.'s.

Discuss each case on the following pages with the other members of your team. Decide whether you will press charges or dismiss the case. Consider the three factors listed in the other column. If the members of your team do not agree, take a vote and decide by majority rule whether or not to prosecute.

After the role-play, discuss the following questions with the other members of your class:

a. What was your decision in each case? What most influenced it?

b. Was it more difficult to decide some cases than others?

c. Compare your decision with the actual decisions made in these cases. Your teacher can tell you what these decisions were.

Case One: Susan Shield

Susan Shield was arrested for the murder of her husband. On March 24, 1975, police answered a call at 1134 Spring Street. They had been told of a family argument in progress. When the officers arrived, the house was quiet and the front door was open. They entered the house and found John Shield dead on the bedroom floor.

A bloodstained dress was found in a garbage can. It belonged to Mrs. Shield. The bloodstains matched Mr. Shield's blood type. The autopsy showed that Mr. Shield had been shot three times in the head at close range. There was no sign of a struggle. A gun was later found two blocks away. It had fingerprints matching those of Mrs. Shield. Tests showed it was probably the murder weapon.

Neighbors told police that John and Susan Shield had had many loud arguments recently. On the night of the murder, they had argued so loudly that the neighbors had called the police.

Susan Shield was arrested at the home of her sister. She was advised of her rights. Mrs. Shield then denied killing her husband. She claimed she had spent the night at her sister's home after telling her husband that she was leaving him "for good."

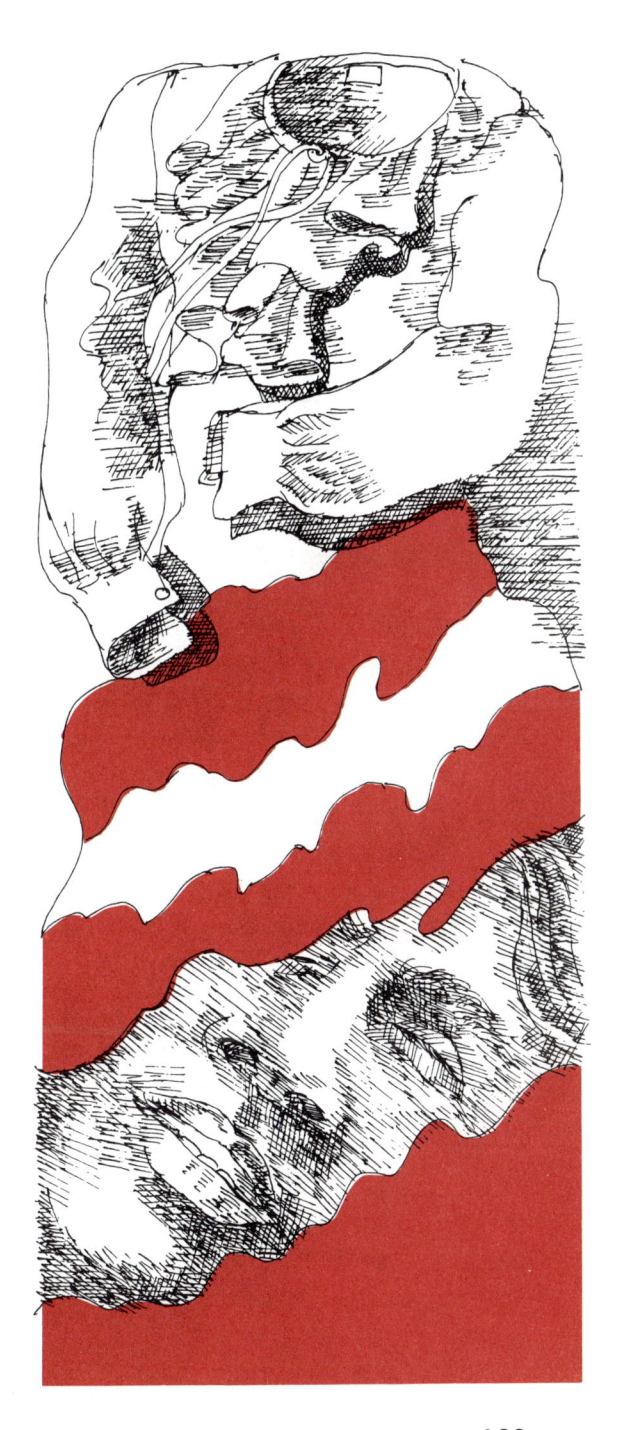

Case Two: public nudity

Ten nude sunbathers were arrested for indecent exposure. The police had received many complaints about nude sunbathers on a local public beach. It is against the law to sunbathe in the nude on a beach. When the police arrived at the beach, they found 10 people there in the nude. The police arrested all 10. The bathers were told to cover up. They were then taken to the police station where they were booked for indecent exposure.

Case Three: Fred Tarton

A club near Brookdale College held a party which ended in a drunken brawl. A policeman at the party in plain clothes saw Fred Tarton punching Harold Kay. The policeman broke up the fight, but Kay's nose was bloody and appeared to be broken. The policeman arrested Tarton for assault and battery, read him his Miranda rights and took him to the station house.

The next day, Harold Kay was questioned. Kay said that Tarton had made an obscene comment to his date. Kay told the police he then told Tarton to shut up. Tarton became enraged and broke Kay's nose.

During questioning, Tarton claimed that Kay was drunk. Tarton said Kay had tried to make a pass at his girl friend. Tarton claimed that he was forced to protect his date by pushing Kay away. This caused Kay to punch him. Tarton said he only hit back after Kay had first hit him. Witnesses at the party claimed they hadn't seen what led up to the fight.

2. What does a defense lawyer do?

The right to have the help of a lawyer when you are accused of a crime is a recent one in the history of the justice system. In the U.S., defense lawyers were first hired by some defendants around 1775. But it was not until the 1960's that the Supreme Court ruled that every person accused of a crime, whether rich or poor, had the right to have a defense lawyer.

Most defense lawyers work for a fee. They are hired by citizens to defend them in court. Sometimes, however, the work of defense lawyers is carried out by public defenders. They work for the government, defending people who cannot afford to hire a private lawyer.

Whether a defendant has hired

a private lawyer or uses a public defender, the job of the defense attorney is the same. Before a trial, the lawyer tries to get the charges against his or her client dropped or reduced. At trial, the defense attorney tries to have the client found not guilty. Or the lawyer may try to show that something which happened at the time the crime was committed made the client's actions less serious.

For example, the lawyer could try to show that the client was mentally ill. The defense lawyer may also try to delay the trial against the client.

Even if a client is found guilty, the defense lawyer does not quit the case. The lawyer must now try to get the client as light a punishment as possible. The lawyer may ask the judge to impose a short sentence.

Thus the defense lawyer must get his or her client the best possible results in any legal way. The role of a lawyer is always to work for the best interests of the client.

Resource person. You may wish to invite someone from the public defender's office or a private defense attorney to visit the class and discuss his or her work and law as a possible career.

3.
Lawyers and ethics

How can you be sure of getting a lawyer who is both honest and able? The answer is, you can't be sure. The work of lawyers is usually not completely understood by their clients.

If a lawyer makes a mistake or acts in an unprofessional way, the client may suffer. Yet clients may not understand why they are being hurt. For this reason, the conduct of lawyers is controlled directly or indirectly by an arm of the state government.

To become a lawyer, a person must pass an examination and be licensed by the state where he or she wishes to practice. The highest court of each state must make sure that lawyers follow proper standards of behavior. A lawyer who violates the rules may be punished by a state court.

Over the past decade or so, there has been a great deal of concern about the conduct of lawyers. This arose out of the Watergate investigation of 1973, which revealed crimes by lawyers in the executive branch of the federal government. As a result, many law examinations now include questions about ethics or conduct.

Here are some sample questions from an ethics examination. Try to select the answers which show the best conduct on the part of a lawyer. Your teacher can tell you which of the answers are considered correct.

a. You are a well-known lawyer. One of your best clients, Tom Smith, has asked you to recommend his son, Bob, for admission to the State Bar (an organization of lawyers). You do not know Bob, but you have known his father for the past 20 years. What should you do?

(1) Do the best you can for Bob since you have known his father for so many years. (2) Check on Bob's background, character, and education and recommend him if he is qualified. (3) Do not recommend Bob because there is a conflict between your duty to your client and your duty to the justice system.

b. You are an attorney on your way home from your new job with a law firm. You stop at a roadside restaurant because of an unexpected rainstorm. In the restaurant you notice that a senior member of the law firm, Bill Jones, is having a drink with a juror on the case that Jones is currently trying. You are aware that it is a serious offense for a lawyer to speak to a juror about a case he is trying. Which of the following should you do?

(1) Return to your car and pretend you did not see anything. (2) Caution them about talking about the case. (3) Inform the judge trying the case.

c. You are an attorney, and your client is asking you to represent him in a divorce case. You know that most attorneys are charging $500 for a divorce of this type. Since your client is new in town, doesn't know the going price, and is wealthy, you charge him $1,000. Is this ethical?

(1) Yes, because each attorney can determine his or her own price. (2) No, because the fees that are set cannot be set so high as to shock other lawyers. This is a shocking difference in price. (3) Yes, the client can always shop around if he doesn't like the price.

Your Turn

1. What is meant by *ethics*? Why is it important for lawyers to be ethical in their practice of the law?

2. Can you think of other ethical issues that lawyers might have to face? Give two examples, and describe what you consider the right decision in each. Explain why you think each decision is correct.

Field Activity

Would you like to be a lawyer? Consider the following questions about yourself: What qualities, talents, and interests do you feel you have that might make you enjoy working as a lawyer? Have you other qualities, talents, or interests that would make you dislike working as a lawyer? If so, what are they?

What information would you like to find out about law schools and the work of lawyers? Write down your questions. Plan to discuss them with a lawyer who visits your classroom, or in a field interview. Can you think of other ways to find this information?

Chapter 11
The Trial

Each person who takes part in a trial represents a special interest and has a special job to do. The judge presides over the trial. The accused person and his or her lawyer are present. The state is represented by the prosecutors. Members of the community, who must have had no contact with the case, sit as jurors. They make a judgment about the facts presented to them. Witnesses — people who have some knowledge of the case — are called to testify. The back of the courtroom may be filled with spectators. Reporters may describe the events in the courtroom for those who cannot be present. Thus a trial concerns the whole community.

A trial is not an isolated happening. It is an important event in our society. In this chapter you will look at the workings of a trial. And you will have a chance to run your own "mock trial" taking the roles of participants in a murder case.

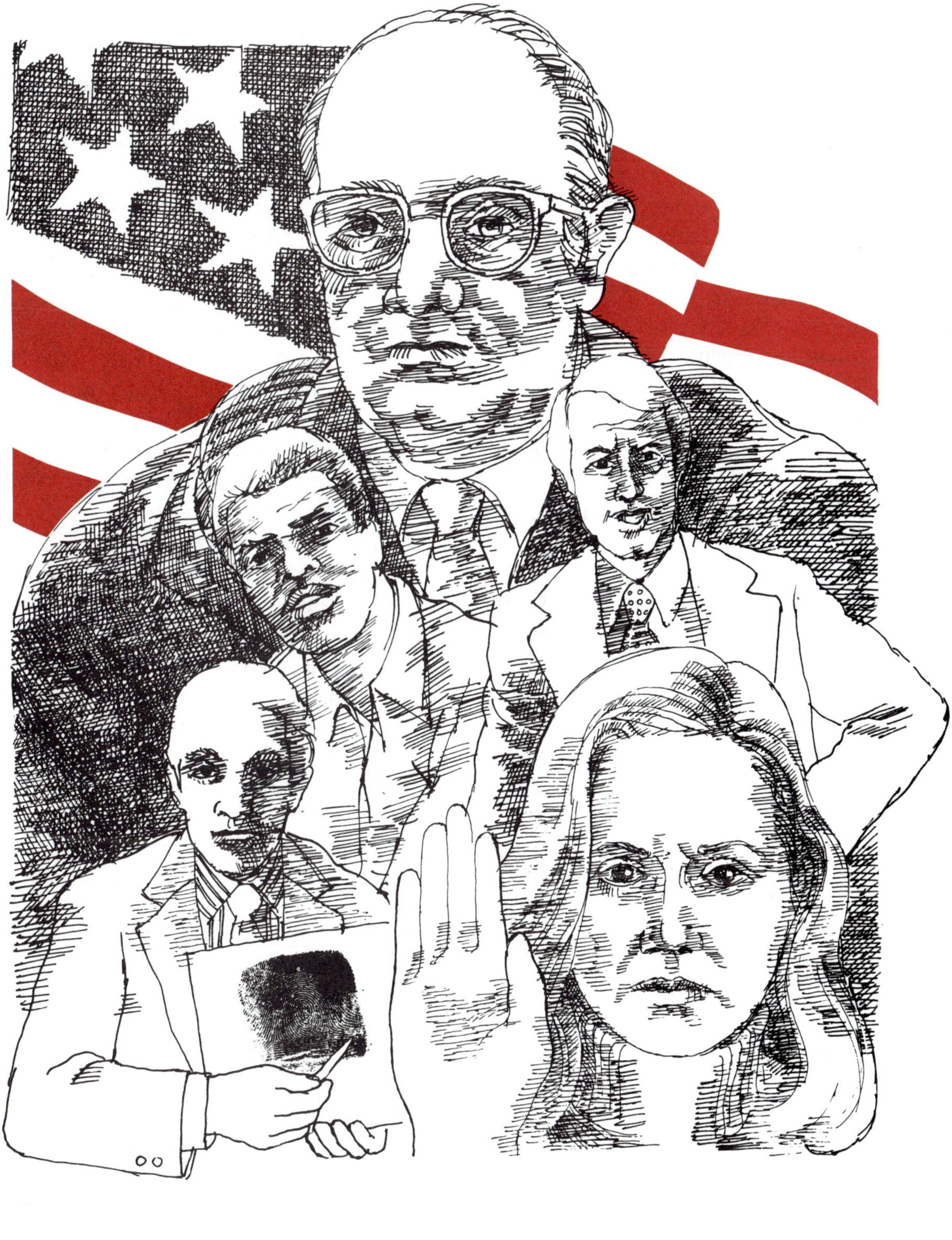

1.
How is a jury chosen?

If two different juries listened to the same case, would they both reach the same verdict?

Our legal system does not allow us to find out the answer to this question using real juries. However, studies have shown that "juries" given the same set of facts do *not* always arrive at the same verdict. Not everyone can be fair in all situations. For example, a juror whose brother was killed in a holdup might not be able to be fair to a person accused of another holdup.

How fair a jury is depends very much on *who* sits on the jury. Thus the choosing of a jury may be the most crucial event of the trial.

Members of a jury come from a group of citizens who have been called for jury duty. The selection process goes something like this: One by one, possible jurors are asked to sit in the jury box in front of the courtroom. The judge and the defense and prosecuting attorneys ask each juror questions designed to show whether he or she can judge the case fairly.

Each lawyer selects jurors the lawyer believes will be most favorable to the case. The lawyers also try to dismiss those who might favor the other side. However, there are certain rules that prevent the process of jury selection from going on endlessly.

Lawyers may reject people as jurors by "challenging" them in one of two ways. A *challenge for cause* can be used against any person who shows that he or she cannot be a fair juror in the case. For example, a juror might say he or she knew the defendant personally, or already believed the defendant was guilty. The juror could then be challenged for cause, and the judge would excuse him or her from the case.

There is no limit on the number of challenges a lawyer can make for cause. However, the challenge will lead to dismissal only if the judge agrees that the juror is likely to be biased.

In addition, lawyers may make a limited number of challenges without cause. These are known as *peremptory challenges*. Lawyers make such challenges against jurors who they feel may be unsympathetic to their side. For example, suppose a lawyer is defending a man who speaks in an extremely sloppy manner. The lawyer might decide to challenge a juror whose speech is very precise and correct. No reason need be given for a peremptory challenge.

Once enough jurors have been selected, the judge swears them in. Then the trial begins.

2. What is evidence?

If you bought a TV and the seller claimed you stole it, how could you prove that you bought the set? One way is to show your sales receipt or your check. This is an example of using *evidence* to show the truth about a question of fact: Did you steal a TV set?

Evidence simply means the ways that are used in a trial to show the truth about a question of fact. (Did Jason Smith murder his landlord?) Evidence can include the testimony of a witness, a letter or other written document, or an object, such as a gun. For example, your sales receipt is written evidence that you bought — and did not steal — the TV. No other evidence is needed to show the set is yours.

If you did not have a sales receipt for your TV, this fact might suggest you stole it. However, this fact alone would not be enough to *prove* that you had stolen the TV. More evidence would be needed. For example, suppose someone said he saw you climbing out a window of the TV store one night, lugging a large box. This would be pretty strong evidence that you stole the set.

Evidence not allowed in court

Not all evidence can be used in court. Very strict rules exist about the kinds of evidence that are acceptable in a trial. The following types of evidence are not allowed:

• *Rumors.* Statements like, "Everybody knows that John beats his wife all the time."

• *Public opinion.* Statements like, "Everybody on the block believes John shot his wife."

• *Biased views.* Statements like, "John is a creep." "John is an angel." "John was always a nice boy."

• *Hearsay.* Statements like, "Bill said that John admitted shooting his wife." Hearsay is a statement made by a witness who is repeating what he heard someone else say, not what he actually saw or heard himself. There are many forms of hearsay evidence. Some hearsay is allowed into evidence under certain circumstances.

• *Irrelevant statements.* Statements like, "John is a good carpenter." Irrelevant statements

that's the one

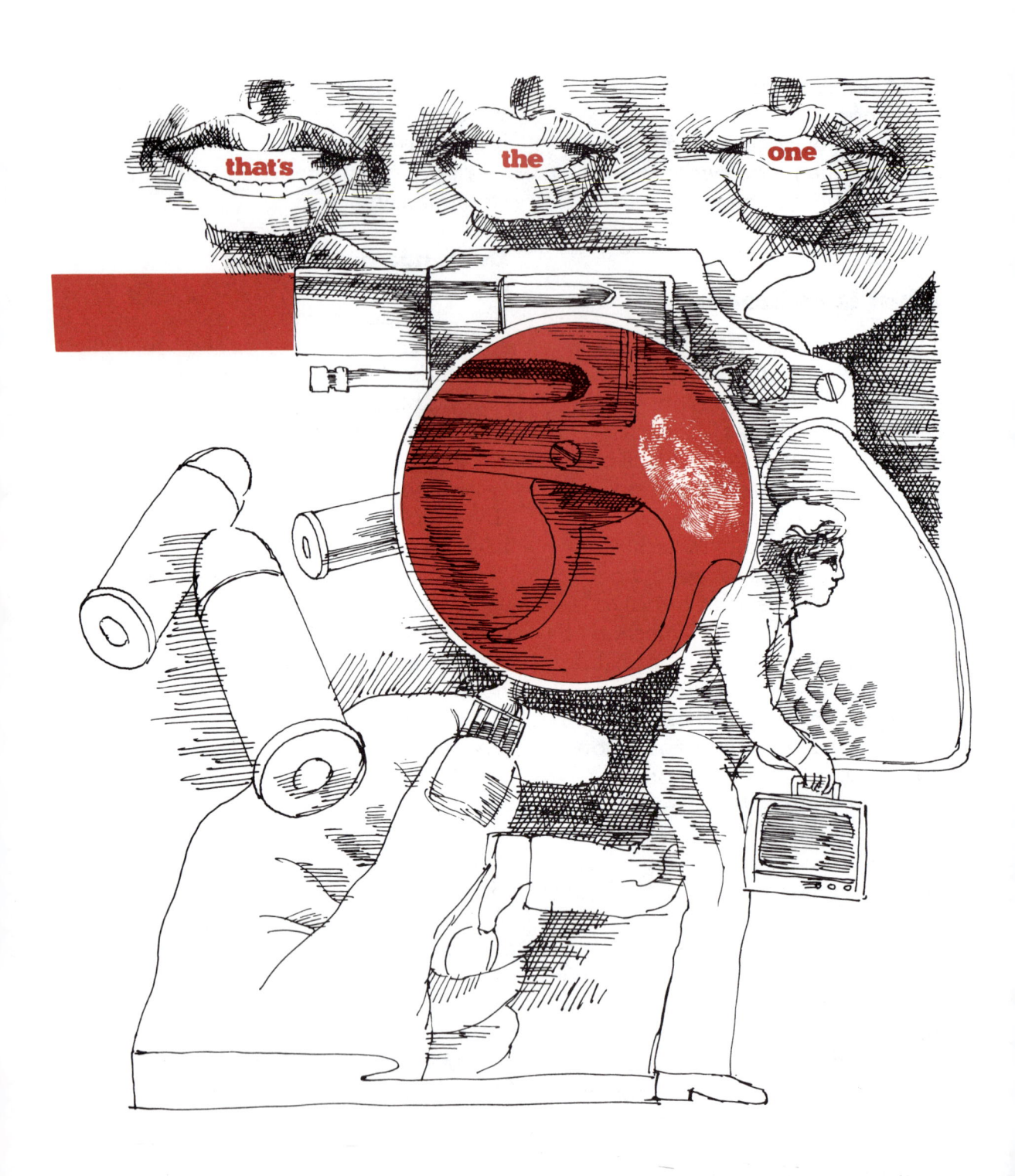

are statements which have nothing to do with the case.

- *Illegally obtained evidence.* For example, suppose the police break into John's house without a search warrant and take a gun. They then claim that John used the gun to shoot his wife. Even though the claim may be true, the police obtained the gun during an illegal search so it cannot be used as evidence.

You be the judge

Assume you are a judge. Based on the rules of evidence, decide which of the following statements or objects you would allow as evidence in your court.

a. During a murder trial, a witness says that he heard strange noises in his neighbor's house at about the same time that a murder took place there.

b. A witness states that the defendant in a grand theft, auto trial was known in his neighborhood as "a no-good bum."

c. The district attorney wishes to show the jury a confession by the defendant. The confession was obtained after 15 hours of questioning by the police.

d. A witness makes this statement: "A friend of mine told me that Sam [the defendant] held up a liquor store."

e. An apartment house manager testifies about a tenant who is the defendant in a burglary case. The witness says that the defendant was always late with his rent and never seemed to have a steady job.

Discuss your decisions with the other members of your class. Do others agree or disagree?

3. What it means to be a witness

It was just about dusk when Ellen finished her job as a waitress at Pete's Coffee Shop. She hurried because she had to walk two blocks to Main Street. There she would catch the bus that would take her to night school. She walked quickly, thinking about her shorthand test that evening. She was confident because she had studied carefully.

Suddenly a young man stepped out of a darkened doorway toward Ellen. She thought she recognized him from school. Before she could say anything, he grabbed her. She screamed and tried to fight him off, but he pulled her into an alley and raped her.

"If you say *anything* about this," he warned, "I will come back and kill you." He ran out of the alley. Ellen was terrified.

Seconds later, another young man approached Ellen. "What happened?" he asked. "I saw a guy run out of here and I heard you scream."

"I'm hurt," Ellen sobbed.

"We'll get help," said the stranger.

Police questioning

The passer-by, Dave Soto, called the police. When two officers arrived in a patrol car, they took Ellen to the emergency room of a nearby hospital. There she was treated for her injuries.

Later that evening, Ellen talked to the police. She tried to answer all of their questions. "I think I would recognize him, but I'm not positive," she said.

A few days later, a sergeant from the police department telephoned Ellen. "Can you come to the station and look at pictures of suspects?" he asked.

At the police station, Ellen picked out a picture of a young man who looked like the one who had raped her. Ellen was not positive about it. However, later that day, Dave Soto also picked out the same young man's picture.

It wasn't until three months later that Ellen was called to appear as a witness at the trial. It seemed a long time to wait. However, she knew that the district attorney had not only to prepare the case but also to find a time when it could be fitted into the crowded court calendar.

At the courthouse, Ellen also saw Dave Soto sitting on one of the benches in the waiting area. After they had been waiting for nearly an hour, a court official told them that they would not be called that day. The lawyer for the defendant had asked that the trial be set for a later date so he could have more time to prepare his case. The judge had granted the request.

Ellen was concerned. "I'm sorry you've had to waste your time," she said to Dave.

Dave smiled. "It's a waste of your time, too," he said. "Anyway, I knew this kind of thing could happen. Don't worry about it. I'll be here when the case is called again."

Finally in court

Six months after the attack, the trial of the young man began. Ellen was the first witness. Again — this time in a courtroom full of strangers — the district attorney had Ellen repeat what happened the night she had been attacked. Her voice shook as she talked. She had never been in court before and the memories of the attack still upset her.

After the district attorney finished, the lawyer for the defendant asked Ellen questions about what she had said. He was unfriendly. He acted as if everything she said was a lie. He suggested that she had encouraged the young man, especially since she had seen him at her school.

The district attorney had warned Ellen to expect this kind of questioning. Although it made her angry, she did not become flustered. She answered the questions calmly.

Next Dave Soto took the witness stand. He said that the defendant was the man he had seen running out of the alley after he had heard Ellen's screams. His testimony too was questioned by the defense attorney. The attorney implied that Dave and Ellen had tried to trap the young man. He suggested that Dave was receiving some "special favors" from Ellen for backing up her testimony.

Conviction

The next day the trial resumed. Ellen was not needed, and she was too busy at the coffee shop to return. She was waiting on tables when the jury returned the verdict of guilty.

Ellen read about the guilty verdict in the newspaper. She was relieved to find that the jury had not been influenced by the hints of the defense counsel. She was even more relieved that the trial was finally over. But at least, she thought, I did my part. She had been a witness and she felt good about that.

Your Turn

1. Summarize the experiences of Ellen and Dave as witnesses. What problems did they face? Do you think witnesses in other cases would face the same kinds of problems? Why or why not?

2. Why do you think Ellen felt good about having been a witness?

Resource person. You may wish to find out more about the experience of being a witness in a court case. One way to find out is through a field visit to your local courthouse. There you might interview witnesses and officials. *Remember, however, that witnesses may be instructed not to talk about their testimony outside the courtroom.*

4.
The elements of a trial

Every crime is defined in a group of laws called the *Penal Code*. Each state and the federal government have a penal code. These laws give us a standard for deciding whether or not a crime has been committed. To be guilty of a crime, a person's acts must fulfill the definition of that crime.

Fact and law

Two kinds of questions are considered at a trial: *issues of fact* and *issues of law*. An issue of fact is a question about what the truth is in a certain case. In a criminal trial, the jury must decide issues of fact. This means that a jury decides what the truth is in the case. When a defendant chooses not to have a jury trial, the judge must decide.

An issue of law is a question about what the law means or what law applies to a case. The judge alone decides issues of law. During the trial, the judge interprets the law. For example, if there is a dispute about whether evidence has been gathered legally, the judge will decide whether or not the police acted properly in the search and seizure of evidence.

Reasonable doubt

Ideally, in our justice system, the defendant is innocent until proven guilty. Another way of saying this is that the prosecution has the "burden of proof" in showing that a defendant is guilty *beyond a reasonable doubt*. Reasonable doubt is one of the keys to our justice system.

Suppose, for example, while standing in front of a bank, you see a masked man go inside with a gun. Moments later you see the man emerge from the bank carrying a money bag. Suppose, further, that you later hear that the bank has been robbed by a masked bandit who had a gun. Though it is possible that the person you saw did *not* commit the robbery, the evidence would lead you to believe *beyond a reasonable doubt* that the person you saw did, in fact, rob the bank. A jury is supposed to be certain beyond a reasonable doubt when, after weighing the evidence, the members feel convinced that the defendant is guilty.

5.
Murder on Line No. 2: a mock trial

In this section, you will use your knowledge of courts as you take part in a mock trial for murder. The facts of the case are as follows:

On the afternoon of November 3, 1983, five young men boarded a bus on Line No. 2 at Central and 8th Streets. Among them was Thomas Ward, age 19. The young men had been to a movie that afternoon and were on their way home. The bus was crowded. The young men sat in different seats near the rear of the bus.

Witnesses do not agree about what happened on the bus that afternoon. Most say, however, that there was an argument over money between the five young men and another passenger, Alvin Fry. Some witnesses report that Fry had argued with the members of the group. Others felt that he was being robbed. In any case, a fight did break out between Fry and the five young men. Other passengers joined in.

During the fight, the bus came to a stop. Passengers began to push toward the exits to escape from the violence. There was panic and confusion.

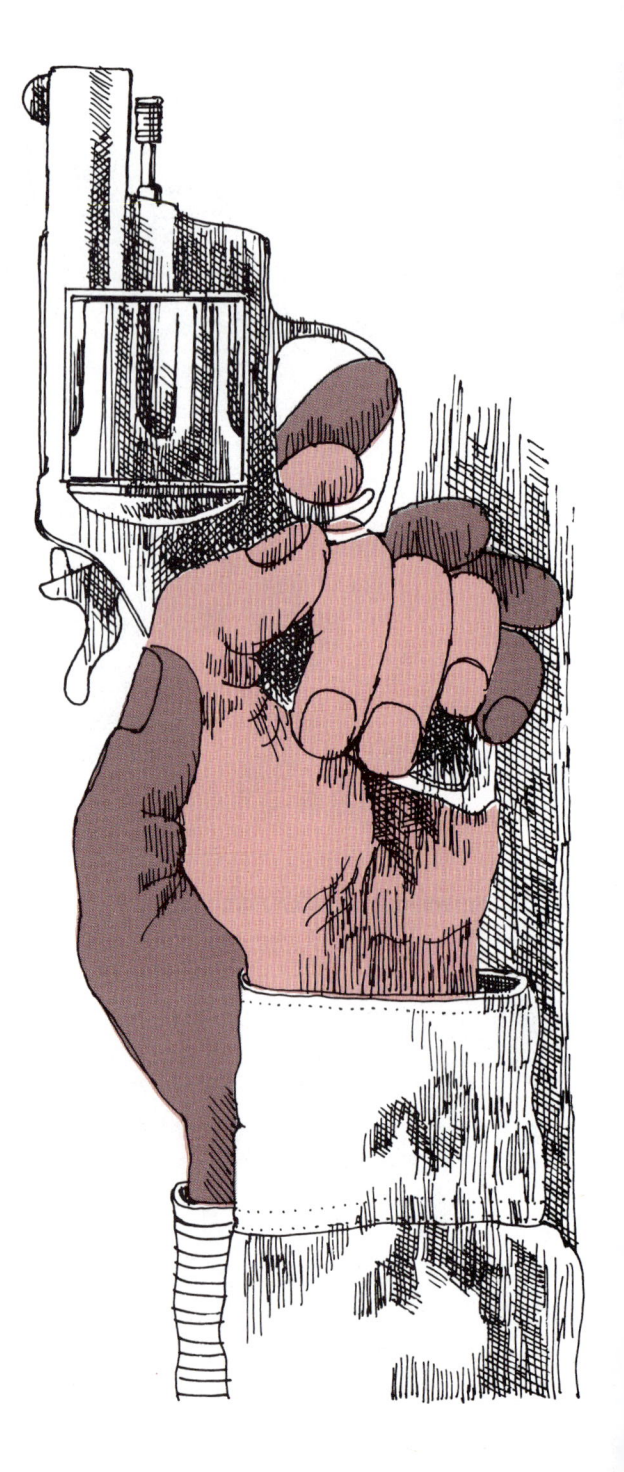

Four of the five young men who were involved in the fight got off the bus. The fifth, Thomas Ward, remained. He was doubled over, holding his side.

Moments later one of Ward's friends pulled a gun. The man was later identified as Peter Brand. Brand shot Fry from outside the bus. Fry was dead upon arrival at the hospital.

Ward and his friends left the scene together. The police later arrested Ward and the others. They were all charged with murder under the state's felony-murder law.

This law states that a person can be guilty of murder even when he or she did not directly commit the murder itself. This happens when there is a murder while another crime is being committed. For example, suppose Smith and Doe decide to rob a bank. Smith knows that Doe is carrying a gun. During the course of their robbery, Mrs. James, a patron of the bank, is shot and killed by Doe. Under the law, Doe *and* Smith are both guilty of murder.

At first, the felony-murder law may seem unfair. However, the idea behind this law is that people are responsible for the results of their actions. In the bank robbery, Smith is expected to know that a gun is a dangerous weapon. Although only Doe carried the gun and fired it, Smith had to know this could happen during a robbery.

Resource person. You may find it helpful to invite a lawyer to visit the class and help with the mock trial.

Staging the mock trial

Now you and the members of your class will have the chance to "try" Thomas Ward for murder. The procedure you will use is called a *mock trial*.

Those who will participate in *People v. Ward* include:

- A team of three district (prosecuting) attorneys.
- A team of three defense attorneys.
- A trial judge.
- Louis Hampton, prosecution witness one.
- Sally Terman, prosecution witness two.
- Elaine Gordon, defense witness one.
- Adam Rivers, defense witness two.
- Defendant Thomas Ward, defense witness three (optional).
- Jury of 12 citizens.

These roles are described in the next few sections.

The district attorney

As district attorney, your job is to show that Thomas Ward is guilty beyond a reasonable doubt of felony-murder. To do this, you will want to show that the following has occurred:

a. Thomas Ward and/or his friends attempted to take money from Alvin Fry against Fry's will.

b. Thomas Ward knew about the robbery and was involved in the attempt to rob Fry when he was killed.

In order to convict Thomas Ward of murder, you must prove beyond a reasonable doubt that *both* of these acts took place.

You will want to question witnesses about Ward's role in the alleged robbery try. This is called *direct examination*. You will also want to question witnesses called by the defense in order to discredit them. This is known as *cross-examination*.

To prove your case, you might want to ask witnesses questions such as the following:

a. Was a robbery planned? If so, did the murder take place as a result of the attempt to rob? (Direct examination of witness Hampton.)

b. Did Ward's actions at the bus stop and on the bus suggest that he planned to rob Fry? (Direct examination of witness Hampton.)

c. Did Ward take part in a robbery attempt against Fry? (Direct examination of witness Terman.)

d. Did Ward threaten Fry? (Direct examination of witness Terman.)

e. Did Ward know of the presence of a gun and of the possibility of its being used? (Direct examination of witness Terman.)

Your team of attorneys should be prepared to do the following:

• Make an opening statement to the court explaining what you believe the facts of the case will show.

• Question your witnesses in order to bring out the facts which support your case.

• Cross-examine defense witnesses in order to weaken the case of the opposing side.

• Make a closing statement to the court stating why you believe you have proved your case.

Louis Hampton, prosecution witness one

As a witness for the prosecution, you will testify to the following facts:

You are 17 years old and a student at Central High School.

About 4:30 P.M. on November 3, 1983, you were waiting at 8th and

Central Streets for the No. 2 bus. About five other young men were waiting there too. The defendant was one of these men.

You heard the men talking about a movie and a gun. One said, "Let's get us some money"; and the defendant said, "Yeah, Ted, you can ask on the bus." Then they all laughed a lot.

When the bus came, they got on ahead of you. You sat near the back of the bus near the victim. One of the young men who was sitting next to the victim asked the victim, "How much money do you have?" The victim said, "None." Then the victim stood up, and a fight started. You observed the five men hitting the victim.

When the bus came to a stop, everyone was pushing and shoving to get off. A lot of people were yelling and screaming.

After you got off the bus, the victim was still standing up inside the bus. The defendant said to him, "You better look out, man." Then one of the men who had been at the bus stop with you put a gun to the window, pointed it at the victim, shot him, and ran away. You saw the victim fall and the defendant run away with the other men who had been at the bus stop.

Sally Terman, prosecution witness two

You will testify to the following facts:

You are 42 years old and work as a high school teacher.

On November 3, 1983, about 4:30 P.M., you boarded the No. 2 bus at 6th and Central Streets.

At the next stop, a group of young men including the defendant got on the bus. One sat next to the victim. The defendant stood up and held onto the overhead railing.

The man seated next to the victim argued with him. He hit the victim. The victim started to get up, but the defendant said to him, "Sit down, man. What's bugging you?" He said something else, but you couldn't hear it. After that, the victim got up and started to move toward the front of the bus. Then the defendant hit him with his fist. A fight started, and more passengers became involved.

When the bus came to the next stop, everyone tried to get off. There was panic. The fight stopped. You got off the bus as did most of the people who were in the fight. You observed, however, the defendant standing in the doorway of the bus. He was looking back toward the victim who was standing in the aisle.

One of the men who had been fighting was standing outside the bus near you. You believe this man yelled to the defendant something about a gun. You decided to get away from there. Several seconds later you heard a shot. You did not look back in the direction of the shot and didn't see who fired the gun.

The defense attorneys

As defense attorney, your job is to show that Thomas Ward is *not* guilty beyond a reasonable doubt of the crime of murder. To do this, you must try to convince the jury of the following:

a. Thomas Ward did *not* attempt to take money from Alvin Fry against his will.

b. Ward did *not* know about the robbery. He was *not* involved in a robbery or an attempted robbery when Fry was killed. Thomas Ward, therefore, cannot be found guilty.

In attempting to show that Ward is not guilty, you might want to ask witnesses about the following matters:

a. Was the discussion of a robbery at the bus stop serious or just a joke? (Direct examination of defendant Ward. Cross-examination of witness Hampton.)

b. Was Ward threatened by

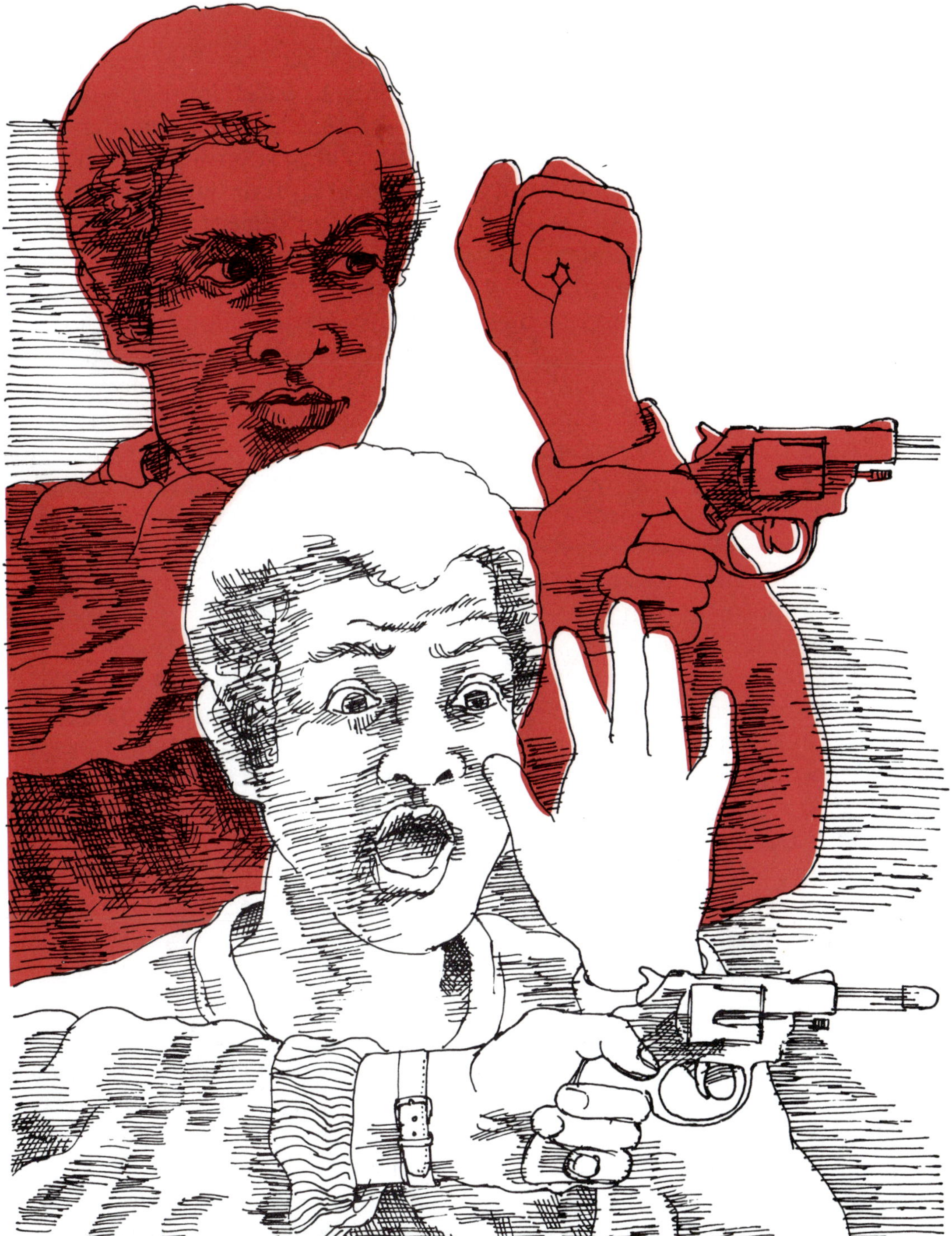

Fry? (Direct examination of witnesses Ward and Gordon.)

c. Did Ward's misbehavior show youthful high spirits that got out of hand? (Cross-examination of witness Hampton.)

d. Did Ward try to prevent a robbery by unloading the gun in the theater? (Direct examination of witness Ward.)

Your team of attorneys should be prepared to do the following:

- Make an opening statement to the court explaining what you believe the facts of the case will show.
- Question your defense witnesses in order to bring out the facts which you believe will support your case.
- Cross-examine prosecution witnesses in order to weaken the case of the opposing side.
- Make a closing statement to the court stating why you believe you have proved your case.

Elaine Gordon, defense witness one

As a witness for the defense, you will testify to the following facts:

You are 35 years old and work as an accountant.

On November 3, 1983, you were sitting on the bus several seats behind the victim. Before the fight broke out, you saw the victim sitting down. Then you saw him standing up and fighting with about five men. You saw the victim hitting them with his hands and kicking them with his feet.

When the bus stopped, everyone started to jump off. You saw one of the men who had been fighting leave the bus and put a gun to the window. The victim tried to duck, but he couldn't. You heard a shot and saw the victim fall.

The man who had fired the gun was not the defendant Ward. Ward was still on the bus at the time the shot was fired.

Adam Rivers, defense witness two

As a witness for the defense, you will testify to the following facts:

You are 24 years old and employed as a deliveryman for a grocery store.

On November 3, 1983, you went to the Palace Theater downtown with Thomas Ward, the defendant, Zach Taylor, Peter Brand, and Ted Stanton. During the movie, Thomas Ward and Ted Stanton were passing a gun back and forth. Ted joked about shooting the gun, and Ward told him to "cool it."

After the movie, the group caught the No. 2 bus. You were

riding in the back of the bus.

While you were on the bus, you heard Ted Stanton ask the victim for money in a loud voice. The victim said he didn't have any money. Ted Stanton hit the victim. Then Ted, Peter Brand, and the victim stood up and started fighting. The victim hit Ward, who was standing apart, watching the fight.

The bus stopped with people screaming and pushing to get out. The back door opened and everyone got off except Thomas Ward and the victim. Ward stood in the doorway, holding his side and looking at the victim. You believe the victim had punched him or kicked him hard in the side. That is why he seemed to be bent over.

You saw Peter Brand standing outside the bus on the sidewalk. He grabbed Ted Stanton's gun from under Stanton's jacket and fired it at the victim. He then laughed and started running. The rest of your group followed him.

The judge

Your role is to preside over the trial of Thomas Ward. You must decide whether or not (a) the attorneys are using fair procedures; and (b) the evidence can be admitted. You should use common sense if you are not sure about the law. The following guidelines may help you.

- Start the trial by naming the case. For example, "The court is now in session. The court will hear *People v. Ward*." Make sure the jury is seated.
- Ask whether the prosecution and defense are ready to present their cases.
- Ask the team of prosecutors to make their opening statement. Then ask the team of defense lawyers to make their opening statement.
- After the defense attorneys have finished, ask the prosecution to call its witnesses.
- After the prosecutors finish questioning each witness, allow defense lawyers to cross-examine each one.
- When the prosecutors finish, ask the team of defense attorneys to call its witnesses.
- After the defense attorneys finish questioning each witness, allow the prosecutors to cross-examine each one.
- After both sides have questioned the witnesses, tell them to make their closing statements to the jury.
- When the closing statements are completed, read the following instructions to the jurors.

Ladies and gentlemen of the jury:

It is your duty in this case to decide the guilt or innocence of the defendant, Thomas Ward. Before making your decision, please weigh carefully all of the evidence that has been presented.

Thomas Ward, the defendant, is accused of murder under the state's felony-murder law. You should keep in mind that no person may be convicted of a crime unless there is proof beyond a reasonable doubt that the defendant has committed that crime.

In order to return a verdict of guilty in this case, you must be convinced beyond a reasonable doubt that:

a. Defendant Ward and/or his friends intended and/or attempted to take money from Alvin Fry against his will and by means of force or fear.

b. Defendant Ward planned to commit the crime of robbery.

If you find both of these points to be true, you may also find Ward guilty of the murder of Fry.

Under state law, the verdict of the jury must be unanimous.

Thank you. Please now withdraw and begin your deliberations. Please select someone to speak for you. Let me know when you have reached a verdict.

Members of the jury

As a jury member, your job is to make a fair decision in the case. You must reach a *unanimous* decision. If you can't agree, you are a *hung jury*. This means you will be dismissed without reaching a verdict. Therefore, try hard to reach a verdict.

6. Appeals

What can defendants do who believe they have been denied their rights? What can they do if they believe the procedures which were followed in their cases were unfair? These matters are called *questions of law*. Decisions on questions of law are often made by *appeals courts*. In this section, you will learn about the work of the appeals courts in the U.S.

What is an appeals court?

During a criminal trial, both questions of fact and questions of law are important. But even after a jury reaches a verdict, a defendant may still appeal the case on questions of law and of fact. The defendant may feel that the law has not been applied fairly to his case. Or he may argue that a constitutional right has been ignored.

For example, take the matter of publicity. A defendant might argue that the case has received too much publicity — that newspaper, television, and radio stories influenced the jurors and made it impossible for them to give a fair verdict. Thus the defendent may argue that he or she has been deprived of a fair trial and should receive a new trial. In such a case, a defendant has raised a question of law. He or she may then take the case to an appeals court. That is a court which decides questions of law.

There are two kinds of appeals courts in the U.S. Each state has its own system of appeals courts. There is also the federal court system. Federal appeals courts decide questions of law which involve federal laws or the U.S. Constitution.

If a defendant loses at one level, he or she may appeal to a higher court. The higher court can decide whether or not to take the case. Sometimes a case begins in a state trial court and is appealed in state appeals courts. If a constitutional point of law is raised, the case may then be appealed through federal courts all the way to the U.S. Supreme Court. That is what happened in the Miranda and Escobedo cases.

147

Chapter 12
Juvenile Justice

Tom Fenten, age 15, threw a rock through a neighbor's window because the neighbor told him not to play baseball nearby. Blake Thompson, age 27, threw a rock through a neighbor's window because he was angry at the neighbor for making noise. Should the juvenile and the adult be treated the same way for this offense?

Mike Phillips, age 16, shot his sister because he was angry at her for ruining his favorite video game. Stuart Smith, age 35, shot his wife because he was angry at her for spending too much money. Should the juvenile and the adult be treated the same way for this offense?

Nancy Byrne, age 14, stole some makeup from a department store display on a dare. Adele Hare, age 23, stole some makeup from a department store because she was tired of paying for things. Should the juvenile and the adult be treated the same way for this offense?

A juvenile accused of a crime is usually not treated the same way an adult would be. Like Laurie in the first chapter, a juvenile enters the juvenile justice system. The aims of juvenile justice differ from those of adult court. In this chapter, you will learn how the juvenile system works.

37

1.
Juvenile justice: does it protect you?

At what age does a person become an adult — 16? 18? 21? In most states, people are said to be juveniles until they are 18. This is very important if you are charged with a crime.

If you are a juvenile and commit a serious crime, you may go to juvenile court. In many states, you might also be taken to juvenile court if you run away from home, if you skip school a lot, or if you have problems which you and your family cannot work out. Thus many of the young people who appear in juvenile court have not been involved in a serious crime.

In juvenile court, you get a hearing, rather than a trial. This means that your case is discussed in front of a juvenile court judge. A hearing is not like an adult jury trial. For one thing, there is no jury. The judge alone decides on your case or problem and also on what to do with you. In most cases, what goes on in the hearing is kept secret from the newspapers, radio, and TV.

In some states, lawyers may prosecute and defend the juvenile. Usually, the police or probation officers tell the judge what you have done or what the problem is. The judge then talks with you and your parents. A psychologist may be called in for advice.

Afterward the judge decides what will happen to you. He or she may let you off with a warning, send you to an institution such as a reform school, or put you on probation.

If you are put on probation, you will probably be allowed to live at home. But you must report often to a probation officer. Among other rules, you must tell the probation officer where you go, what you do, and with whom you spend time. If you break the rules or get into more trouble, you may be sent to an institution.

Problems

There are many problems with the system of juvenile justice. But the system has been improved a great deal in recent years. For example, 20 years ago, young people had few of the rights that protected adults accused of a crime. It was felt that young offenders should not be treated as criminals, and therefore the proceedings should be informal. But, as a result, all kinds of evidence could be used in juvenile court that would have been thrown out of adult court. Juveniles were not guaranteed the right to have a lawyer. They didn't have the right to cross-examine witnesses.

In addition, juvenile judges often had little or no training in working with young people. As a result, the juvenile court often didn't protect young people. It was simply a stop on the way to reform school. The major advance in juvenile justice came with the Gault case in 1967.

The Gault case

Gerry Gault was on probation for another offense when he was accused of making an obscene phone call to a neighbor. Because Gerry was 15 years old, the case went to juvenile court.

Gerry was placed in a juvenile center without any notice being sent to his parents. His parents were told on one day that his hearing would be on the next day.

At the hearing, Gerry was not told he could have a lawyer. He had no chance to question and cross-examine the neighbor who had complained of the phone call. Gault had to testify against himself. No notes were taken. When the hearing was over, Gault was found guilty.

The juvenile court ordered Gault to go to a state school for boys. Under state law, Gerry could be kept at the state school until he was 21. That could mean up to six years in the school. An adult found guilty of the same crime could have been sent to the county jail for only 30 days and fined from $5 to $50.

Gault appealed his case to the Supreme Court. He said it was unfair that juveniles did not have the same rights to defend themselves that adults had. He also complained that juveniles could receive more severe penalties than adults for the same offense.

In May 1967, the Supreme Court ruled 8–1 in Gault's favor. The Court said juvenile justice procedures had to be changed. It said that young people charged with delinquency had many rights, including the following:

a. To be notified of charges and the dates of court hearings.
b. To have the help of a lawyer.
c. To cross-examine witnesses.
d. To remain silent.

Since the Gault case, the U.S. Supreme Court has made other key decisions affecting juveniles' rights. In one case, the Court ruled that juveniles, like adults, can be found guilty only if their guilt is "beyond a reasonable doubt." In another case, however, the Supreme Court held that juveniles, unlike adults, do not have a right to trial by jury.

Your Turn

What arguments can you make in favor of treating juveniles the same as adults accused of a crime? What arguments can you make against treating juveniles the same as adults? Which side do you believe has the stronger arguments?

2. Should we have juvenile courts?

In recent years, many people have criticized juvenile courts. They say that young people should get all the rights of adults in the courtroom. They say that young people should have the right to a jury trial. Some think that juvenile court judges have too much power and still lack adequate training. "One person shouldn't be allowed to decide if you are innocent or guilty," a lawyer said recently.

In some states, juveniles do have virtually the same rights as adults except that of a jury trial. Yet many people believe that the differences between juvenile and adult courts help protect young people. They say a juvenile court judge can take the time to listen to the young person in trouble. It is better to have the young person and his or her family talking about the problem with the judge than to have two lawyers arguing it out.

Moreover, most juvenile court hearings are kept private, while adult trials are reported in the media. In an open trial, a young person in trouble could have his or her name ruined for the rest of his or her life. For these reasons, many people would like to keep the juvenile courts different from adult courts.

Justice system interview: in juvenile court

Steve Lachs is a juvenile court commissioner. He acts as both judge and jury in juvenile hearings. If a minor is found guilty in one of Lachs's hearings, the juvenile is then said to be delinquent. A delinquent is made a *ward* of the court. This means the court has the right to decide the best way to help the juvenile.

Describe a typical day in your hearing room.

Most cases I see are either

grand theft, auto, or joyriders. I also deal with runaways, burglaries, vandalism, curfew violations, drunk driving.

Do you think runaways belong in court?

I don't think they belong in juvenile court, which is as close as you can get to a criminal system. But there must be some way for society to deal with these kids. Sometimes parents want the kid in court because they feel they can't handle the child. And it isn't always the kid's fault. I've seen any number of cases where, after talking to, seeing, and listening to the parents, there is no doubt in my mind why the kid ran away.

Do you feel the juvenile court system is doing its job?

I'm not convinced we are really doing as much as we can with kids to rehabilitate them. Some of the failure is due to lack of money and personnel. And from what I see in court, little emphasis is placed on what happens to the kid. As far as I can see, a lot more of the system is devoted to deciding guilt or innocence than to trying to help a kid.

What would you do if you were the parent of a youth who was accused of committing a minor crime, such as shoplifting?

I would want to cope with it

rather than let the court do it. Proper parents can do a lot better job than the court. But often the parents just aren't up to it. At that point, society — through the juvenile court — has to step in.

What about the minor who commits violent crimes?

Some people are unhappy with the basic idea behind the juvenile court. The whole philosophy is rehabilitation, not punishment. I'm not sure that philosophy was developed with a mind for a 17½-year-old, 6′ 3″, 180-pound kid who has not gone to school for a while and who commits armed robbery. I wonder if you were to ask people about the armed robber, if they wouldn't want him punished.

What worries you most about the juvenile justice system?

The inefficient way the cases are handled. It's very bad for society to put a kid through the following: He or she is observed committing a burglary, chased, arrested, detained. Finally, he or she is brought to court for the day of reckoning. But because no witnesses have been called, there is no evidence against the kid. He or she is freed and leaves. I fear the lesson that the kid has learned about the judicial system. It might have been better if he or she had never been arrested. Then the kid would at least still have a fear of being caught at a crime.

Resource person. You may wish to invite someone experienced in juvenile justice to visit your class to discuss the system. Consider asking questions such as the following:

a. What kinds of cases do you see most often in your courtroom?

b. Is it true that violent crimes among youths are increasing? What percent of your cases, would you say, involve violence? How do you think these crimes could be stopped? Do you think violent juvenile offenders should be processed in the same court system with those charged with minor offenses?

c. Do you think minors should be given the right to jury trials, if they choose?

d. How well does the juvenile justice system work? Does it help young offenders correct their behavior or does it — as some people say — make them into better criminals?

e. In what ways do you think the juvenile justice system could most easily be improved?

3. David and the public defender

Assume that you are a public defender in a juvenile division. Your job is to defend juveniles who cannot afford their own lawyer. As a lawyer, you have a professional duty to defend all persons who are assigned to you to the best of your ability.

Your supervisor in the public defender's office has assigned you to defend David, age 17. David has been accused of shooting to death a 16-year-old boy. Before interviewing David, you look up his past juvenile record:

By talking to police officials you also find out that David is a leader of a violent youth gang.

Now you interview David. During this interview, David is arrogant. He says to you: "Listen, I'm a juvenile. I can get away with this. Juvenile court is a pushover." He also tells you, "That guy wasn't worth anything." He brags that his friends will "help out" with any witnesses to the shooting. You try to explain to David that the charge against him is very serious. He cuts you off saying, "Stop all that counseling stuff." Then David looks you straight in the eye and says, "I want you to get me off. That's your job."

Age	Offense	Disposition
9	runaway	released to parents
10	truancy	released to parents
11	shoplifting	released to parents
12	shoplifting	released to parents
13	bicycle theft	found to be delinquent by juvenile court; placed on informal probation
14	assault (school)	placed on informal probation for three months
15	illegal possession of a firearm (.38 cal. pistol)	probation violation; probation extended an additional three months
16	assault and robbery (elderly shopkeeper beaten)	sent to forestry camp for six months

Your Turn

1. As the public defender in this case, what are your feelings? Is David right? Is it your job to "get him off"? Or do you have a responsibility to see that he gets proper guidance? What other responsibilities might you have in this case?

2. How will you handle David's case? Will you (a) defend David to the best of your ability? (b) refuse to continue as David's public defender? (c) do something else?

4.
When should a juvenile be tried as an adult?

Three youths strolled along the sidewalk on a busy downtown street. They glanced in store windows and talked among themselves. They seemed full of energy. Then one pointed to an old man walking just ahead of them. The old man walked slowly and held his coat around him. The youths approached him.

"How 'bout some money, old man," said one of them.

The old man looked frightened. "Sorry, boys, I don't have any today," he replied.

"Don't go out without your money," said another youth as he pushed the old man to the sidewalk.

The three youths began to kick the old man. He couldn't fight back. Passers-by looked frightened. Some tried to stop the attackers. Others hurried away.

"Get the police!" someone yelled.

The youths ran away. The old man lay on the sidewalk very still. He died the next day in the hospital.

Is this an unusual incident? Not according to experts on juvenile crime. They say that young people today are committing more violent crimes than ever before. Statistics show that more and more juvenile crime involves murder, rape, armed robbery, and other crimes of violence.

The growth in violent crime by young people has caused strong public concern. Some people put part of the blame on the juvenile justice system. "Lock them up and try them as adults," is a common cry.

These demands raise an important question: *Should juveniles accused of serious and violent crimes be tried as adults?*

Under our present system, it is possible, in many states, for juveniles to be tried in adult courts. When a juvenile is

157

accused of a serious crime in these states, the district attorney decides whether to ask the judge to try the juvenile as an adult. If the district attorney finds there is sufficient cause, he or she asks for a *fitness hearing*. During this hearing, the district attorney explains to the judge why he or she thinks the accused should be tried as an adult. Then the defense attorney gives reasons why the accused should be tried as a juvenile. After hearing both sides, the judge makes a decision.

The decision as to whether a juvenile should be tried as an adult often depends on the following questions:

a. How serious was the crime? A serious criminal would probably not be aided by the juvenile justice process.

b. What is the juvenile's age? Is he or she close to the age at which accused persons are treated as adults?

c. What is the juvenile's previous history as a delinquent? Is this his or her first crime?

d. Can the young person be rehabilitated before he or she comes under an adult court? Or have there been previous attempts to rehabilitate him or her?

Toward a Better System of Justice

In this part, you have had the chance to look at many aspects of the adult and juvenile court systems. No doubt you have become more aware of the strengths and weaknesses of the court system.

Now it is time to consider what you have learned.

- List those practices which you think ought to be changed in both the adult and the juvenile court systems.
- List those practices which you think have worked well in the two systems.

When you have finished your summary, answer the following questions:

What changes or improvements in the way the adult and the juvenile court systems operate would you recommend? Which parts of the system should be preserved? Is it possible to make improvements without disturbing what is good in the system?

The Gavel: a Bibliography

Beyond a Reasonable Doubt: Inside the American Jury System
by Melvyn B. Zerman, Thomas Y. Crowell, 1981.
After touching on the historical background of our jury system, this book takes you step-by-step through a trial from jury selection to verdict.

The Controversial Court: Supreme Court Influences on American Life
by Stephen Goode, Julian Messner, 1982.
Discusses landmark rulings and their impact. Also includes profiles of the justices.

Guilty or Innocent
by Anita Gustafson, Holt, Rinehart, & Winston, 1985.
Examines ten of the most famous criminal cases in history, and demonstrates that verdicts can depend on many different variables.

Famous Criminal Trials
by Andrew David, Lerner Publications, 1979.
A dramatic account of famous criminal cases in history, including Sacco and Vanzetti, the Rosenbergs, the Chicago Eight, and James Earl Ray. Discusses the circimstances that spurred each trial, the evidence against the suspects, and the outcomes of the trials.

PART 4
THE BARS
The Problem of Punishment

Chapter 13
The Problem of Punishment

Every crime harms someone in some way. Homeowners may lose their property to a burglar. A clerk may lose his life during an armed robbery. Men and women on the street may be beaten by muggers.

What should we do with these criminals when they are caught and convicted? Should we make them pay back their victims? Or should we punish them as a kind of revenge? Should we keep them in jail so that they cannot harm anyone again?

Should prison be used to try to prevent others from committing similar crimes? Or should prison be used to try to change criminals so they will be able to live in society once again?

Today in America there is little agreement about how to handle criminals. In this chapter you will learn more about how our society punishes criminals and about problems within the system.

Punishment in American history. Above, an 18th century workhouse; next page, below, public flogging and display in stocks were common. Page 164, convicts often had to work late into night on treadmills, with foot power providing the energy to keep machines running.

Your Turn

Write the statements below on a separate sheet of paper. Then mark either "strongly agree," "agree," "disagree," or "strongly disagree" next to each statement. Compare your reactions with those of other members of the class. Keep this paper until the end of the part. You will then have the chance to compare your views before and after studying about punishment.

• Punishment should include making the offender pay back the victim for any money loss that resulted from the crime.

• The death penalty should be abolished (ended).

• The purpose of prison is to rehabilitate (change) criminals.

• Long prison sentences and the death penalty will keep others from committing similar crimes.

• Prison sentences should be made longer to keep serious criminals off the streets.

Resource person. You may want to invite a probation or parole officer to class to discuss the corrections system.

1.
Good intentions, bad results

The story of prisons in the U.S. is one of efforts to make a system that is humane, but still effective. The result, sadly, is a system that often is neither humane nor effective.

In colonial America, prisoners received quick and harsh punishment. Many were put to death for crimes that we today would consider minor. Jailkeepers were often "businessmen" who ran their jails for profit. Inmates had to pay for their own food and other basic needs. Sometimes poor inmates starved to death before their trials.

Regret and remorse

Following the Revolution, Americans began to demand changes in the way convicts were treated. The Quakers, a religious group opposed to war and violence, took the lead in working for reform. They argued that prisons should try to change the behavior of criminals. They said that prisoners should be put in solitary confinement. Then prisoners would be able to think about their deeds and become sorry for what they had done.

The Quakers also introduced other reforms. For example, children were no longer sent to jail. The government also started to provide food and clothing to inmates at its own expense.

The "Pennsylvania System," as these reforms were called, aimed to punish and *correct* those who had broken the law. This new idea for *correction* of criminals was adopted throughout the United States and Europe.

Unfortunately the reforms introduced by the Quakers seldom worked. Prisoners locked up in solitary confinement frequently became sick, went insane, and died.

The work system

The poor results of solitary confinement led prison reformers to call for something new. They decided to put emphasis on work. Under this system, prisoners were allowed to leave their cells and work and eat together.

The work system was widely used and accepted. It still influences prisons today. In many prisons, inmates make such things as license plates and furniture for government offices. Or they may grow food for the prison population and wash the uniforms of hospital employees. These jobs keep inmates busy and save the taxpayers some money. But they do not give the inmate a skill that might be used in the outside world.

Rehabilitation

Following the Civil War, there was a new call for reform. Reformers argued that criminal behavior was like a disease. They felt that inmates should be "treated" in order to improve their behavior toward society. With proper treatment, the reformers said, prisoners would be *rehabilitated*. That is, their character would change and they would be able to take up a normal life.

This idea caught hold in the last part of the 19th century. Offenders began to get schooling, job training, health care, and counseling. When inmates could convince the staff that they were ready for release, they were allowed to leave the prison.

Soon doctors, social workers, and others were treating prisoners in order to rehabilitate them. In addition, many states built prisons to separate less dangerous prisoners, women prisoners, and the criminally insane.

The idea of rehabilitation governs our prisons today. Under it, prisoners learn that to get out of prison early they must attend school, meet with psychologists, and take job training, as well as work at a prison job. Every so often, there are parole-board hearings. At them, prisoners try to show that they are ready to lead honest lives.

Parole-board members use their own judgment and reports by prison staff to decide whether to release prisoners early. Some prisoners do change. Others, however, try to "con" their way out of prison and commit more crimes.

Today a large number of former inmates return to prisons after committing new crimes. This high rate of return suggests that prisons do not change inmates into law-abiding citizens. Americans are once again demanding reforms in the corrections system.

Chartread: recidivism

Today many experts question whether prisons can change the behavior of criminals. Evidence that prisons do not change prisoners comes from many sources. One source is the *recidivism rate*. That is, simply, the number of inmates who violate the law after they are released from prison.

The U.S. Department of Justice performed a study on recidivism rates in 1984. Chart 1 shows the percentage of inmates who are later convicted for committing another crime. Chart 2 shows the recidivism rate by age group for New York State. Chart 3 shows the recidivism rate for persons according to what crimes they originally committed.

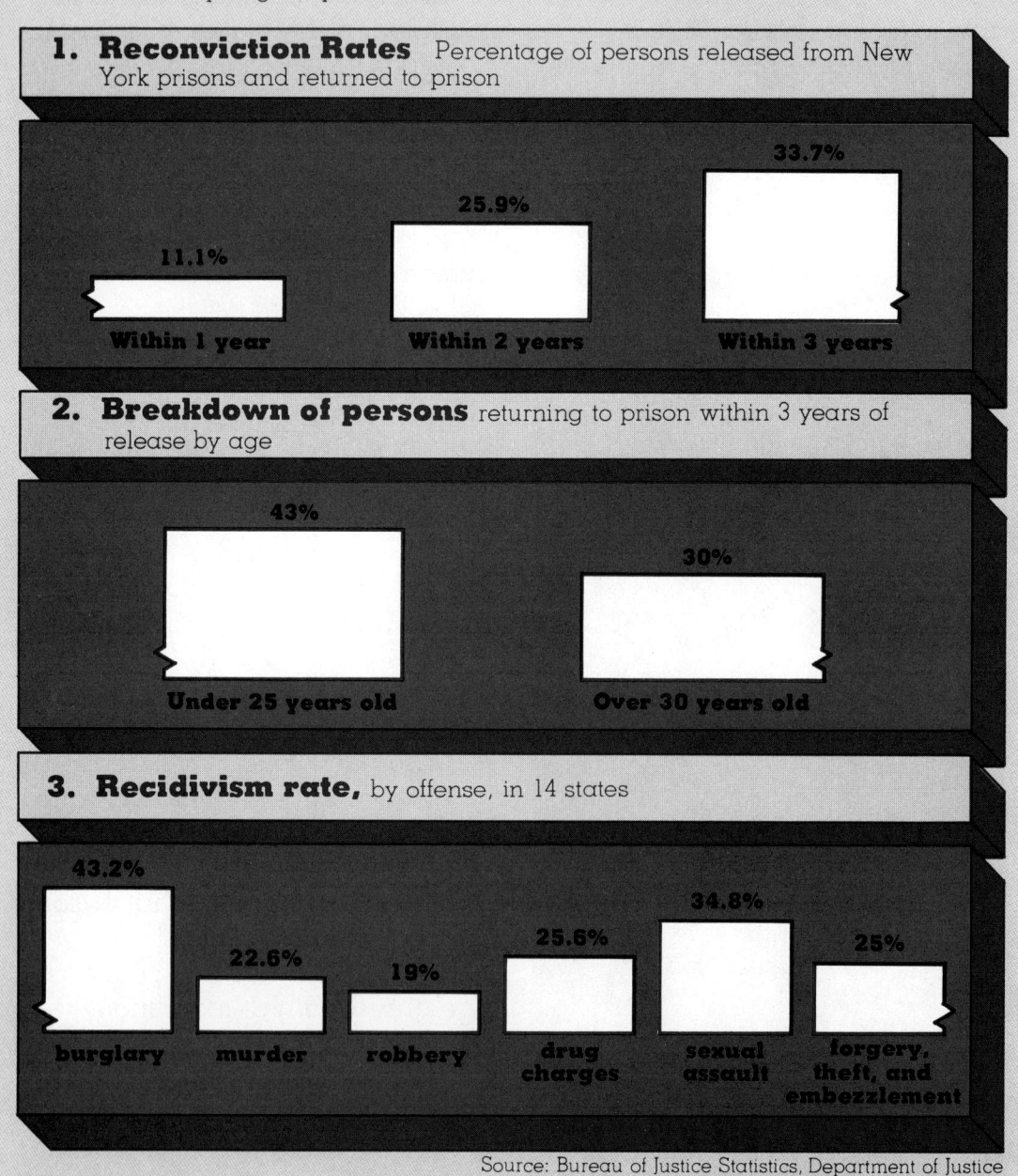

1. Reconviction Rates
Percentage of persons released from New York prisons and returned to prison

Within 1 year	Within 2 years	Within 3 years
11.1%	25.9%	33.7%

2. Breakdown of persons
returning to prison within 3 years of release by age

Under 25 years old	Over 30 years old
43%	30%

3. Recidivism rate,
by offense, in 14 states

burglary	murder	robbery	drug charges	sexual assault	forgery, theft, and embezzlement
43.2%	22.6%	19%	25.6%	34.8%	25%

Source: Bureau of Justice Statistics, Department of Justice

Reform

There are many suggestions for reform in prisons. Some people propose that the use of prisons should be drastically reduced. They say that only a few very dangerous persons need to be locked up. They believe that social and economic problems are at the root of most crimes, and these can therefore be reduced by correcting the problems.

Other reformers do not agree that social and economic problems are the main cause of crime. In their view, prisons will always be needed to keep offenders out of society until they are rehabilitated. However, rehabilitation is possible only if prisons are humane, these reformers say. Thus they want to improve prison conditions.

On the other hand, there is a group of people who believe that prisons can't rehabilitate criminals. These people say that prisons should have other aims. The most important aim is to *punish* criminals. Another aim is to keep dangerous people away from society for a long time. A third is to *deter* (keep) others from committing crimes by showing that the penalties are severe. Many of the experts in this group agree that prisons should be more humane. They also are for releasing prisoners who are not dangerous. But they believe that dangerous criminals should be kept in prison for longer terms.

Your Turn

Summarize the main arguments above. Which of them do you agree with most? Why?

2. Making the punishment fit the crime

When a defendant has been tried and found guilty of a crime, the judge decides what the sentence should be. Many factors go into this decision. They include the past history of the convicted person, his or her attitude about the crime, and the best interests of society. To help make this decision, the judge usually asks the probation department to present a report which recommends a sentence. In addition, the defense lawyer and the prosecutor are given a chance to argue for or against the recommendation of the probation department.

After listening to these recommendations, a judge usually imposes one of the following sentences:

Probation. Release with supervision by a probation officer.

Fine. The convicted person must pay a set amount of money to the court.

Youth training school. For convicted persons up to age 25. Actual time served is set by the state's youth parole board.

State mental hospital. Convicted persons who are insane, sex offenders, or narcotics addicts may be sent to mental hospitals.

County jail. For convicted persons who are sentenced to serve short prison terms — usually up to one year. These usually result from misdemeanor cases, but in some states, persons convicted of less serious felonies may also be sent to a county jail.

State prison. For people 18 or over or for juveniles tried as adults and convicted.

Suspended sentence. A convicted person is released with or without probation.

Sentencing a person: a role-play

This section is adapted from the *Bill of Rights Newsletter* of Spring, 1975. It requires the class to be divided into groups. Each group will role-play a different sentencing hearing.

Members of each group should choose the following roles: judge, defense lawyer, prosecutor, probation officer, or offender. Two or three people may play each role, except those of the judge and the offender.

The defense lawyer(s), prosecutor(s), and probation officer(s) in each group should study the sentencing choices described above and the probation report for the case assigned to their group. Probation reports begin on page 170. Then each group should decide on a sentence to recommend to the judge.

When members of the group are ready, do the role-play as follows:

a. The judge calls on the probation officer to recommend a sentence and the reasons for it.

b. The judge calls on the prosecutor to recommend a sentence and the reasons for it.

c. The judge calls the defense lawyer to recommend a sentence and the reasons for it.

d. The judge may ask questions of any of the role-players during the hearing.

e. When all arguments are completed, the judge asks the convicted person if he or she wishes to say anything. The defendant may or may not wish to make a statement.

f. The judge then announces the sentence.

CASE ONE
Probation Report

Name: Jane Carson.

Age: 21.

Background: Jane Carson is one of 10 children from a broken family. She doesn't know her father and doesn't get along with her mother. Her school grades were very bad. She speaks poorly and cannot read. She has no work skills. She has a long record of drug abuse. Carson has tried to commit suicide four times. She first became pregnant at age 15. She has three children by two different fathers. She is married. Her husband is in jail for assault and for selling dangerous drugs. Carson was sent to state mental hospital several times starting at the age of 11. A social worker recently wrote: "Her whole life seems to have been one of looking around for something or someone to need her as a worthwhile individual."

Prior Record:

Age	Arrest Record	Action by Juvenile Authorities
15	prostitution	probation (1 year)
16	grand theft	placed in a foster home
17	runaway from foster home	committed to state mental hospital for 90 days observation; released
17	grand theft, auto	probation (3 years)
18	burglary	

Age	Arrest Record	Action by Adult Authorities
18	burglary	probation (3 years)
18	theft	probation continued
19	shoplifting	10 days suspended sentence; $35 fine
20	theft	county jail (90 days); attempted suicide and was placed in a state mental hospital; escaped

Current case: After escaping from the state mental hospital, Carson surrendered. Youth authorities sent her to a school for women. Here she had a fight with another woman whom she burned severely on the face with an iron. After the incident, Carson said, "I wish now I had killed her."

Verdict: Jane Carson pleaded guilty to charges of assault and battery (felony).

CASE TWO
Probation Report

Name: Allan Jacobs.

Age: 21.

Background: Allan Jacobs is the oldest of six children. His father was an alcoholic and a gambler. His parents were divorced in 1977. Jacobs dropped out of high school before completing the 11th grade because of failing grades and truancy. He has an average I.Q., but the few jobs he has held have not lasted long because he has been arrested so often.

Prior Record:

Age	Arrest Record	Action by Juvenile Authorities
17	possession of dangerous drugs	probation
18	under influence of dangerous drugs	counseled and released

Age	Arrest Record	Action by Adult Authorities
19	possession of marijuana	county jail (180 days) — sentence suspended; 3 years probation
19	burglary	county jail (30 days) plus one year probation
19	assault with a deadly weapon	released; victim refused to prosecute
20	grand theft, auto; hit and run while under influence of drugs	committed to Youth Training School (paroled after 12 months)

Current case: Three months after his release on parole from the youth training school, Jacobs was arrested for armed robbery during which he took an automobile. Jacobs pleaded guilty to the robbery charge. He said he took the car because "I needed a ride home." He claims he never had a gun, but only pointed his index finger inside his shirt so that it looked as if he had a gun. No gun was found by the police when Jacobs was arrested.

Verdict: Guilty of armed robbery (felony).

CASE THREE
Probation Report

Name: Dave Riley.

Age: 24.

Background: Dave Riley had a relatively normal childhood and upbringing. He has an above-average I.Q., and earned above average grades in school. He was graduated from high school and attended junior college for two years. He is married and has one child, a son. He has no record as a juvenile offender. His record as an adult offender is short and generally minor except for his most recent arrest.

Prior Record

Age	Arrest Record	Action by Adult Authorities
21	receiving stolen property	case dismissed for lack of evidence
22	drunk driving	county jail (10 days) — suspended sentence; $150 fine
23	sale of stolen property (3 TV sets)	county jail (6 months) — suspended sentence; 3 years probation

Current case: Riley and a partner stole an automobile and got police badges and handcuffs from a pawn shop. Posing as police officers, Riley and his partner entered a liquor store, got the confidence of the owner and then held him up for $2,000. Two days later, the pair tried the same thing again, but were captured while carrying out the robbery. Riley has confessed to his part in the two crimes. He said he had to raise $16,000 quickly because of financial difficulties in his failing TV repair business.

Verdict: Riley pleaded guilty to one count of armed robbery, one count of attempted armed robbery, and one count of grand theft, auto (felonies).

Debriefing

a. Hold a class discussion of each case. The judge in each group should explain the cases to the class. Describe the sentence that was given and the reasons for the sentence. List each sentence on the board.

b. Do any members of the group or class object to any of the judges' decisions? If so, why?

Outcome

Your teacher can tell you the actual decision made in the courts in each case. They are on page 44 of the teaching guide for this book.

How were the classroom sentences similar to and different from the actual courtroom decisions?

Chapter 14
Behind Bars

What is it like to live behind bars? It is an unpleasant experience. Life in prison leaves a mark on people long after they return to the outside world. In this chapter, you will learn more about what happens to a person in prison. Below is an account of life in Attica prison in New York State. Attica is a maximum-security prison for men. This means it is for prisoners who are thought to be dangerous. As you will see, prison life not only restricts a prisoner's activities. It also deeply affects his or her mental and physical condition.

1.
The life of a prisoner

A prisoner enters Attica wearing shackles and leg-irons. He is given gray prison clothes. Then he is fingerprinted, given a number and a haircut. He goes to an isolation cell for two days, 24 hours per day.

After the two days, he takes a series of interviews and tests. Finally he is assigned a job and transferred to a regular cell block.

The cells are about six by nine feet with seven-foot-high ceilings. The nearest window is across the

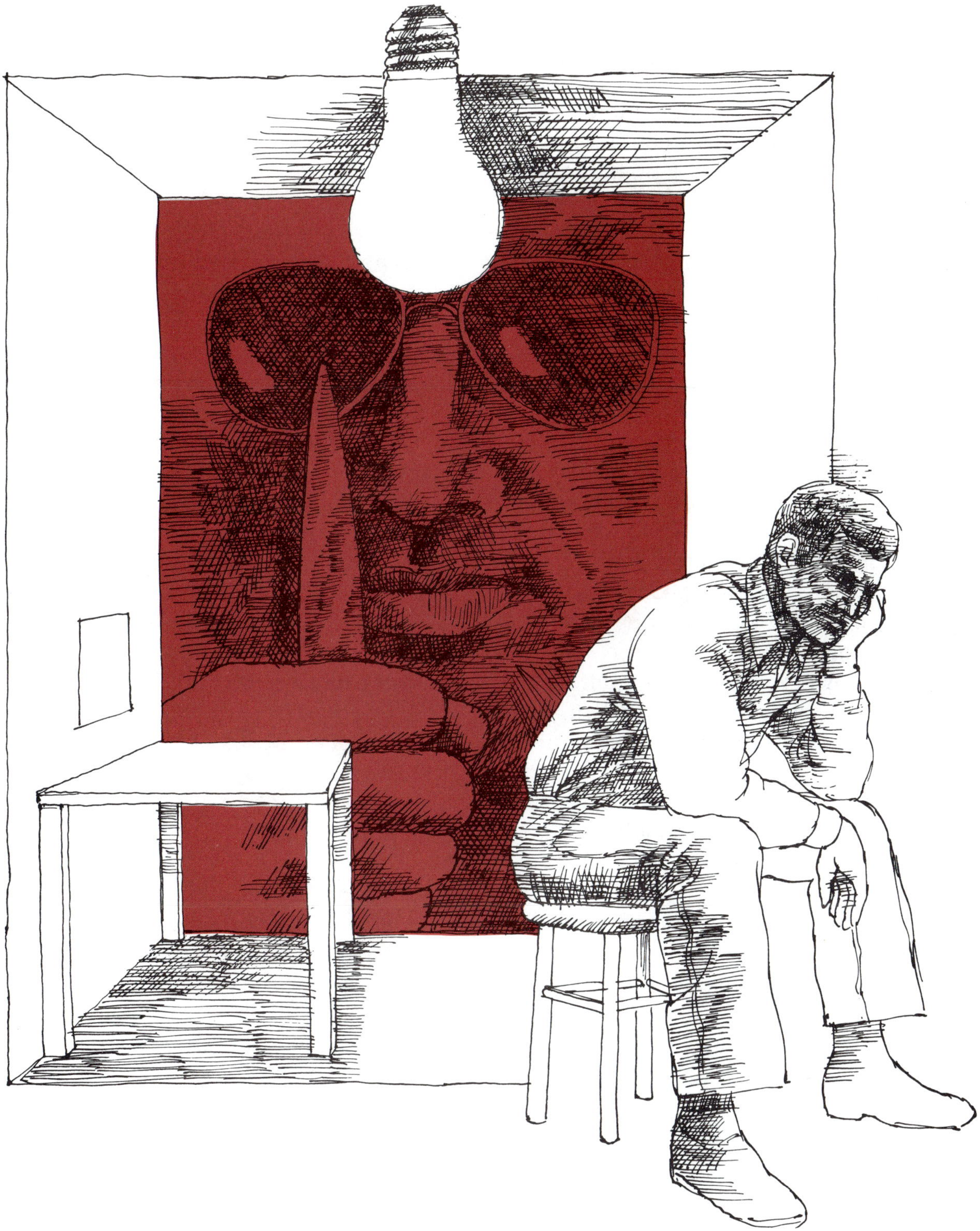

corridor. Each cell has a bed, a metal stool, a small table, a two-drawer metal cabinet, earphones for the prison radio system, a toilet, and a sink that runs cold water only. Light comes from a bare 60-watt light bulb. While in prison, an inmate spends 14 to 16 hours a day alone in his cell.

During weekdays the daily routine begins at 5:50 A.M., and ends at 6:30 P.M. Talk between cells is allowed until 8 P.M. After that, prisoners must be silent. Lights go out at 11 P.M. The radio system goes off at 12 midnight. From inside the cell, the only way a man can look up or down the gallery is with a mirror.

An inmate's life is controlled by hundreds of rules. His mail may be read. His radio programs may be screened. His reading materials may be controlled. He is expected to work at a prison job that may pay between fifty cents and six dollars a day. If he has a visitor, he must talk to that visitor through a steel mesh screen. Before and after the visit, there is a strip search. He has to remove his clothes and a guard probes every opening of his body.

The prisoner may be the victim of threats and various kinds of attacks by other prisoners. This is especially likely to happen if he is weak or young. It is difficult for the guards to protect everyone at all times.

Gangs add another violent element to prison life. Gangs often form among men of similar ethnic backgrounds. Violence in prison life often grows out of conflicts between gangs. In fact, some prison officials believe the only way to control violence is to provide separate areas for different gangs.

Not all prisons are like Attica. Some offer much better conditions. However, most persons convicted of serious felonies are likely to face the kind of prison life just described.

Resource person. This section is adapted from the *Bill of Rights Newsletter*, Spring 1975. After you read it, you may wish to invite a parole officer and/or ex-convict to visit the class.

Your Turn

1. Select a corner of your classroom. Use masking tape to mark off an area nine feet long by six feet wide. Then use the tape to mark off an area large enough for a bed, a stool, a table, a two-drawer cabinet, a toilet, and a sink. Imagine spending 14 to 16 hours each day locked in this

area. What are your feelings and thoughts? Write them down.

2. What practical considerations are involved in giving prisoners more space, better facilities, and more freedom to move about? To what extent do you think prisoners' living conditions should be improved?

2.
Prisoners' rights

If you were a prison warden, what sorts of rules would you make to control prisoners? Would guards be allowed to search prisoners' cells or read their letters? Would inmates be allowed to read books in which the hero is a criminal? Would inmates be allowed to go to the doctor for any reason, even a headache? Would punishment be used on prisoners who did not obey? If so, what kind?

Until the 1960's, the prison warden could make almost any rules he wanted. Courts often refused to hear cases involving inmates' rights. The courts said that inmates could be handled in any way that prison officials saw fit.

Thus prison officials had almost total power over the lives of prisoners. In many cases, the law inside the prison walls was made by prison officials. As a result, beatings and solitary confinement became common ways to keep prison discipline.

During the 1960's, there was an increase in prison violence. This violence made the public aware of the question of prisoners' rights. The courts changed their attitudes toward prison conditions. They began hearing prisoners' rights cases.

Recently many courts have begun pointing out rights which people possess even after entering prison. They have also listed some rights a prisoner does *not* have.

The U.S. Supreme Court has said that a person must lose many rights when he or she enters prison. This means that prison inmates keep their rights only when those rights do not conflict with the goals of the prison.

What are the goals of a prison? According to the U.S. Supreme Court, these are the three most important:
- to protect society from the criminal;
- to rehabilitate the inmate;
- to maintain security and order in the prison.

In dealing with prisoners' rights, the Court must strike a balance. On the one hand are the rights all citizens have. On the other are the goals of the prison.

Censorship in prison

The fine balance between prisoners' rights and prison goals can be seen in the question of censorship. For example, can prisoners' mail be censored? This is important to prisoners because mail is one of the few contacts they have with the outside world. Many prisoners feel that they should have the right to send and receive letters without having them first read by prison officials.

Prison officials argue that they must read prisoners' mail for security reasons. They say that prison mail must be checked for illegal materials such as drugs, weapons, escape plans, or other evidence of trouble.

In 1971 a federal appeals court held that in most cases, prison authorities may not censor *letters to the courts*. This decision allows prisoners to write to judges about general prison conditions. But prison officials still have the authority to *read* such letters before they are mailed.

A related question is whether prisoners have the right to be interviewed by newspapers and magazines. The court ruled that prison officials can make their own decisions whether or not to allow interviews.

Your Turn

1. What are the arguments in favor of censoring prisoners' mail? Against censoring prisoners' mail?

2. Why might the issue of censoring be important to prison inmates?

3. Look up the rights set out in Amendments I, II, and IV of the U.S. Constitution. Which of these rights, if any, do you think prisoners should *not* have? Explain your answer.

Chapter 15
Probation

People who are convicted of crimes are not always sent to prison. There are many reasons for this. One reason is that prisons are overcrowded. Many judges don't want to add to the problem by putting someone in prison who may not be dangerous. Also, young people who commit crimes are often put in the care of their parents. Many judges feel that putting young people in reform schools may lead them into a life of crime. Thus judges often use probation, rather than prison or reform school. In this chapter, you will learn more about probation.

Resource person. After reading this chapter, you may wish to invite a probation officer to visit the class to discuss the problems of probation.

1.
What is probation?

A person who is convicted of a crime may be placed on probation. This means that the offender continues to live in the community, but has to follow certain rules. Thus people on probation can continue to support themselves and their families. Young people on probation may remain at home. Or the judge may put them in a foster home, probation camp, or school.

Probation works this way. After a person is found guilty, a probation officer interviews the person and others who know him or her. The officer then recommends to the judge whether or not to grant probation.

If probation is granted, the judge sets rules. If a person violates these rules, he or she can be ordered back to court. The judge may then decide to cancel probation. If so, the person can be sentenced to a term of confinement instead.

2.
Justice system interview: probation officer

"Since I'm a drug testing officer, all my contacts with my clients have to be on a surprise basis. I contact people in the office or their homes or on their jobs. Sometimes we meet at someone's house or a restaurant. I go out quite a bit. My theory is that you don't know what's going on until you get out there on the street and see where it's coming from.

"Yesterday, I found that I had two people whose tests showed that they had been using heroin. I have to get these people into the office to find out how much heroin they have taken and what to do about it.

"If the drug use is out of control, I'll try to get them into a hospital or a drug program. I'll try to get them off the street one way or another. Somewhere along the line I have to make a decision about what to do with a client.

"Naturally you have to get them drug free one way or another. This can mean going to jail. But usually there are several choices besides jail. You put them into a hospital. You let the judge know what you're doing. If a person is a threat to other people, you get him into a position where he no longer is a threat.

"When I get back from lunch, the office is usually full. I talk to spouses and parents of people in jail. They wonder how their

Probation: A probationer, standing, meets with two officers.

relatives are doing. I study some new cases coming up. A lawyer calls me about what I intend to recommend on a certain case. I write another report and by now it's 3:30 P.M.

"The first person whose tests showed he was on heroin comes in. Not only is he back on heroin, but he's gotten arrested in someone's home for burglary. A new offense takes away a lot of your choices. I tell him I can recommend to the judge that he either goes to jail or gets into a drug treatment program. He takes the drug treatment program.

"Around four, my clients start coming in. I take urine specimens and do skin tests. The urine test only works if the drug has been used in the last three or four days. But a needle mark stays on for three or four weeks. I have a magnifying flashlight and I look at the veins in their arms. You become very skilled at knowing how a person uses drugs.

"Most of the people on probation are just average people. But there are some on probation who are hardcore, repeat offenders. I like to work with this kind — the heavy offender, the one who's been in trouble a long time.

"I like crisis. I'm a good problem-solver. My work is different, exciting. It gives me a chance to have a lot of contact with people. I was born and raised on the streets. I like the streets and I like the people. I like doing something a lot of people can't do."

Resource person. You may wish to invite a probation officer who works with young people to visit the class.

Your Turn

Here are some questions you might ask a probation officer. After reading them, think of three further questions to ask.

1. What do you do during a typical day? How much time is spent on paperwork? On personal contacts?
2. What do you like most about your work?
3. What do you find most frustrating in working with people?
4. What do you feel you are accomplishing with your work?
5. Do you feel that the corrections system works well? If it doesn't work, can you pinpoint where it goes wrong? How might it be put right?

3. Who is a delinquent?

Have you ever committed any of these offenses?
- thrown rocks at people;
- damaged a park bench, a street sign, or other public property;
- broken a fence, a window, or other private property;
- trespassed on someone else's property;
- wandered around a railroad yard or tracks;
- loitered at a street corner;
- broken into an abandoned building;
- shoplifted anything;
- slipped into a movie theater or other place of entertainment without paying admission;
- walked off with a supermarket trolley;

- beaten someone up;
- hit one of your parents;
- used alcohol, marijuana, or any other drug;
- used someone else's car without permission, even though you returned it;
- disrupted class at school;
- attempted to get married without your parents' consent.

Some of the offenses above are very serious. Some are not. But if you are under 18 and have committed *any* of the offenses listed above, you *could* legally be considered a juvenile delinquent in most states. Today a delinquent is a young person who, according to the court, (a) has committed a delinquent act and (b) is in need of treatment, supervision, or rehabilitation.

Your Turn

1. If you have committed any of the offenses listed above, were you ever caught? If yes, does that make you a delinquent? Why or why not?

2. Are there any acts on the list which you feel should *not* be called *delinquent*? If so, why?

You be the judge

Assume the role of a juvenile court judge. Today you will decide whether three youths in

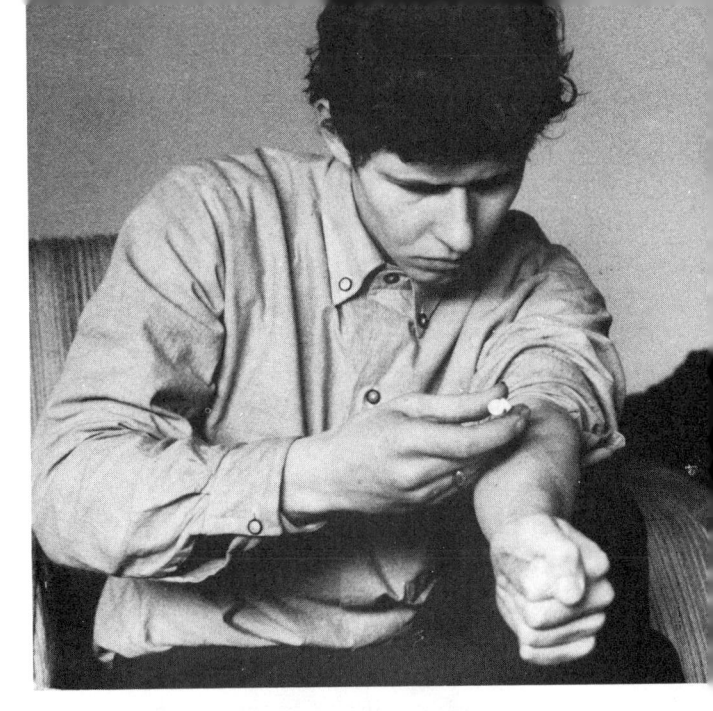

Some delinquent acts are very serious, and some are not.

separate cases are delinquent. All three are 15 years old. They have been brought before the court on charges that they stole automobiles. In each case, the judge has found that each of the youths *did* steal a car for the purpose of joyriding. Joyriding, when committed by an adult, is a misdemeanor. As the judge, you must now rule on whether any of the boys is delinquent. If so, how will you deal with the case?

Case one: Ron Adams. The probation officer says this is Ron Adams' first time in court. Local police have not had previous contact with Adams. He has a B average in school and is a minor discipline problem. Since Ron's arrest, his father has made an effort to spend more time with him. Ron's parents have disciplined him, and Ron seems to have accepted this punishment well.

Case two: Robert Mendez. The probation officer reports that this is the first time Mendez has been in court. Mendez' father is not living at home, and Mrs. Mendez is raising the family by herself. She works as a practical nurse. Robert failed the ninth grade and attends summer school. School authorities say that he is not a discipline problem. Mrs. Mendez feels Robert is a "good boy" but he just "won't do what he is told." She says she could use some help.

Case three: Paul Carter. The probation officer reports that Paul has a previous record for running away. Paul's father died last year. There are six children in the family. Paul is the youngest and the only one left at home. He has a very high I.Q., but his school records show poor grades. He has been transferred four times in high school. He is now going to a special school for students who have been in frequent trouble in regular schools. His mother says that since her husband's death she has had to work to support herself and her family. She finds it difficult to control Paul.

Your Turn

1. What factors did you take into consideration in making your decisions?

2. What questions might you ask the probation officer to help you reach your decision in each case?

3. Which, if any, of the above youths did you rule were delinquent?

4. Do you think that young people who commit the same delinquent acts should always be treated the same way? Why or why not?

Chapter 16
Parole

In about one fourth of the states today, inmates can be released from prison if a parole board believes they have been rehabilitated. Who should be paroled? How should they be chosen? Should we have parole at all? What happens to people who have been paroled? In this chapter, you will learn more about these questions.

Resource person. You may want to invite a parole officer or member of a parole board to visit the class to discuss parole and the corrections system.

1. What is parole?

In many states today, a person sent to prison is usually given an *indeterminate sentence* by the judge. This means that the person is not sentenced for a set number of years. Instead he or she is given a minimum and maximum term. For example, a person convicted of robbery may be given a sentence of one year to life, or "one to life."

How long that person remains

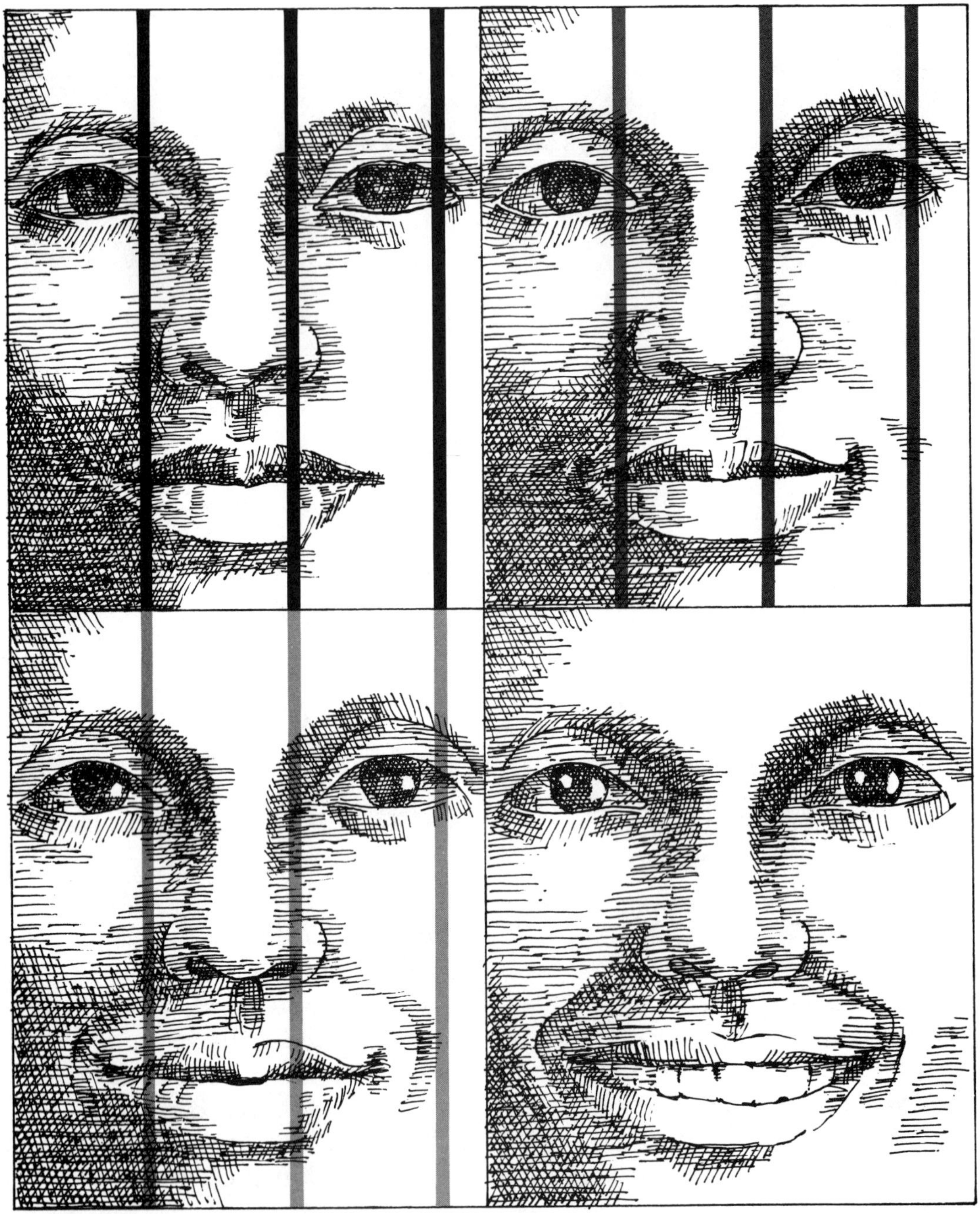

behind bars is up to the parole board. For example, a person sentenced to "one to life" may be required by the parole board to stay in prison for a term of five years. Suppose the convicted robber was imprisoned on January 1, 1983. His parole board decided he must remain in prison for five years. His release date will be January 1, 1988. However, the prisoner may be released *earlier* than 1988 if the parole board grants him parole.

Prisoners released on parole are called *parolees*. Usually a parolee must obey certain rules set by the parole board. These rules often require that the parolee report to a parole officer, and stay out of trouble. The parolee who violates the rules can be sent back to prison.

2. The parole board game

In this game you will have the chance to role-play a parole board hearing.

Divide the class into groups of six students each. Members of each group should choose one of the following roles to play: three prisoners (Jane Carson, Allan Jacobs, and Dave Riley) and three parole board members.

Each prisoner should read his or her own case history and prison report. (Case histories will be found on pages 170–173 in this book. The prison reports begin on the next page.) After studying their case history, each prisoner in the group should plan what he or she is going to say to the parole board.

The parole board members should write down questions they wish to ask the prisoners. After all cases have been heard, the parole boards should decide whether or not to grant paroles.

1. What decisions did each board make in each case? What were the reasons for these decisions?

2. Case one involves a woman prisoner. Based on what the parole boards reported to the class, do you think she was treated differently than the male prisoners? Why or why not?

3. A parole board member once said. "We have this terrible power. We sit up here playing God." What do you think he meant by this? Write your answer in one paragraph.

Peer teaching. This game is adapted from the *Bill of Rights Newsletter* of Spring 1975. It can be used in peer teaching. If you wish to peer teach this game, make arrangements with your teacher.

CASE ONE
Prison Report

Name: Jane Carson.
Sex: Female.
Age: 23.
Marital status: Married (husband in prison).
Current case: Assault and battery. Sentenced to state prison for women for 2–5 years.
Time served: Two years.
Parole board action last year: Parole denied.
Work-school record: Assigned to laundry where she had a poor work record due to faking illness numerous times. Started second-grade reading program, but failed to progress.
Prison staff report: Reported several times for violating prison rules. Can be pleasant at times, but gets angry easily. Makes enemies among other inmates. No hobbies or worthwhile use of leisure time. Attempted to commit suicide with a kitchen knife.
Psychologist report: Carson is still disturbed and dangerous. She knows she needs help, but refuses to cooperate with the program here.

CASE TWO
Prison Report

Name: Allan Jacobs.
Sex: Male.
Age: 23.
Marital status: Unmarried.
Current case: Convicted of armed robbery. Sentenced to a minimum-security state prison for 5–25 years.
Time served: Two years.
Parole board action last year: Parole denied.
Work-school record: Assigned to auto repair program where

he developed a good work record. Did not appear motivated to learn. Took two high school courses (English and math), but failed both because he didn't do assigned work.

Prison staff report: Reported five times for violating prison rules. (All for fighting with other inmates.) Appears to be sullen and angry much of the time. Does not get along with other inmates or prison staff. Appears to have a "chip on his shoulder."

Psychologist report: Jacobs is quiet in group counseling session and refuses to talk about his problems. He appears to have no concept of the rights and feelings of others.

CASE THREE
Prison Report

Name: Dave Riley.
Sex: Male.
Age: 26.
Marital status: Married, one child.
Current case: Armed robbery; attempted armed robbery; grand theft, auto. Sentenced to a minimum-security prison for five years to life.
Time served: Two years.
Parole board action last year: Parole denied.
Work-school record: Assigned to work in prison dairy where he developed a good work record. Took college-level courses.
Prison staff report: One report for fighting with another inmate. Very cooperative with prison staff but is not sincere at all times. Often rejected by other inmates. He spends his leisure time studying and writing letters to his wife and child.
Psychologist report: Attended all group counseling sessions but seemed to be trying to "psych out" the psychologist. Riley does not seem to feel that his crime was a serious one. He constantly complains that prison is a waste of his time.

3.
Fixed sentences

In recent years many states have done away with indeterminate sentencing. In its place, they have adopted what is known as *fixed* or *determinate sentencing*. A fixed sentence is a set term a prisoner must serve for a crime. Fixed sentences differ from indeterminate sentences in several important ways. For example, under fixed sentencing:

- The range of time to be served is very narrow and set by law. For example, a person convicted of assault with a deadly weapon might receive a sentence of two to three years. In indeterminate sentencing, that term might be one to 15 years.
- The prisoner must be told *at the time of sentencing* or shortly after *exactly* how long he or she will be in prison.
- Persons convicted of the same crime serve about the same amount of time.

Under fixed sentencing, a convicted person's sentence is based on the type of crime he or she has committed. Other considerations make little or no difference.

Many prison reformers favor fixed sentencing. They point out that, under the old system, two people convicted of the same type of crime might serve vastly different amounts of time in prison. Reformers feel that this is unfair. It often makes convicts feel frustrated and angry.

Your Turn

1. What advantages might fixed sentencing have for a convicted person? What disadvantages?

2. What prison term do you think a convicted person should serve for (a) armed robbery, (b) the sale of hard drugs? Give reasons for each choice.

3. Based on what you know about fixed and indeterminate sentences, which system do you favor? Why? Write your answer in one or two paragraphs.

4.
Staying out

Many former convicts find it hard to stay out of trouble after they are released. Former convicts have special needs. Programs have been developed to help them. One such program is the Seventh Step Foundation. It works both with prisoners who are about to be released and with former convicts trying to keep from returning to crime. All Seventh

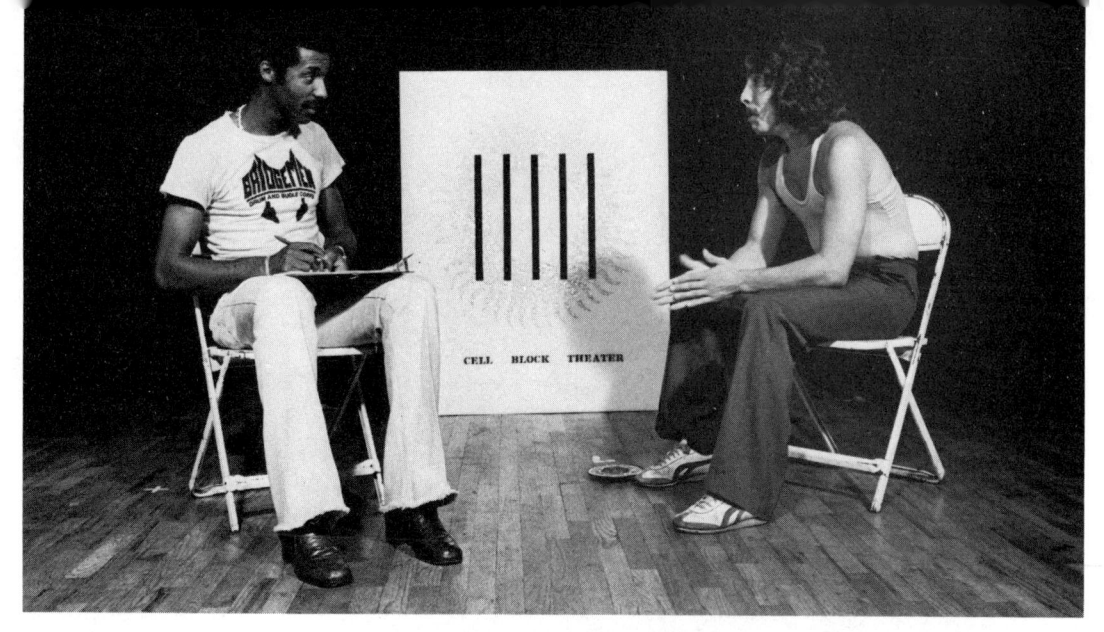

Staying out: *Former convicts in Cell Block Theater act out an encounter between an angry tenant and a superintendent. "It helps you get used to people," says one ex-convict. Next page, other former convicts sharpen their skills in English as a way of coping with the outside world.*

Step staff members are ex-offenders themselves.

The following case study is real. It is the story of a man who is in the Seventh Step program.

"When I was very young, my parents put me in an orphanage because I had serious heart problems and they could not afford to get me help. I got into trouble so I was sent to reform school. This is where I got my first education in crime. I learned that stealing was not wrong. It was a way of life. From reform school, I went to the state prison with a five-year-to-life sentence for murder and armed robbery.

"When I left prison, they gave me $25 and a suit of clothes. I was out three days and I robbed a bank and a hospital. Then I robbed places all over the country. Finally I was caught for armed robbery and got another five-years-to-life sentence. It cost me another eight years of my life. This time I went to a maximum-security prison."

Living in the real world

"When I left prison I felt totally helpless and frightened. I didn't know how to talk to a lady, how to take a lady out, or how to dress. Fitting into society is a real problem. You have a feeling you want to make up for lost time. It's hard to sit still even for five minutes.

"As far as adjusting to society, I

preventing
prefix
presenting
preparing
precede
preach
PREEN
PRE-MONITION
SEED
PRE

don't know how long it will take. For me, getting in my car and coming to work is a thrill. To go to the refrigerator and get a drink is a great feeling for me. I've only been out four months. That's a small amount of time compared to 21 years in prisons and reform school. The adjustment period is not over, and I don't have any more chances. Next time I'll be sent away for the rest of my life."

Thoughts on crime
"I've been a thief all of my life. For me, it is easy to be bad and it is a struggle to be good. I could go out and, just like that, get money. It's my profession. It's illegal — but it is the only thing I am good at — so far.

"Getting a job is a special problem. How do you tell someone you've been in prison 21 years? How do you tell them you've been arrested for murder? How do you tell these things and then expect them to give you a job?

"When I got out of prison, there was no program for people like me. Then I found this Seventh Step Foundation. I was also lucky to get married right away. These two things are saving me and holding me together.

"I can see that I can help someone and someone cares about me. With my experience, I think counseling juvenile delinquents and other ex-offenders is the only job I qualify for. I would hate to imagine what would happen to me if I lost my job and my wife.

"I tell myself every day, 'I can make it, I can make it.' This period of my life, I am happier than I have ever been. During these four months, I have done a lot of fighting within myself to come this far. I never knew I had any good qualities until now."

Peer teaching. This section is designed for peer teaching. If you wish to peer teach this chapter, make arrangements with your teacher.

Your Turn

1. What is the Seventh Step Foundation? What is its aim?

2. How would you describe the man who tells his experiences in this section?

3. What is his attitude toward stealing? Do you agree that he was a "success" at stealing? Why would he have this attitude?

4. How does he react to the freedom of being out of prison?

5. In what ways does a program like the Seventh Step Foundation's help released prisoners?

Chapter 17
Youth Behind Bars

How should society deal with young people who are put behind bars? This is one of the toughest problems in the juvenile justice system. Many experts believe that locking up young people does more harm than good. In this chapter, you will learn more about the problems in the juvenile justice system. You will also learn of a state's experiment in closing its reform schools and how this has affected juvenile crime rates.

Resource person. You may wish to invite a youth corrections officer, probation officer, or parole officer to visit the class and discuss the youth corrections system.

1. Training camp

Danny was a bright but troubled boy. After a series of violent acts, Danny was found delinquent by a juvenile court judge. He sentenced Danny to three months in a training camp. Danny had to say good-bye to his mother and brother. He would be held in a cell overnight and leave on a bus in the morning.

There were about 20 other boys on the bus, but Danny didn't know any of them. Danny had never been away from home before and he was scared. He wondered how the other boys felt.

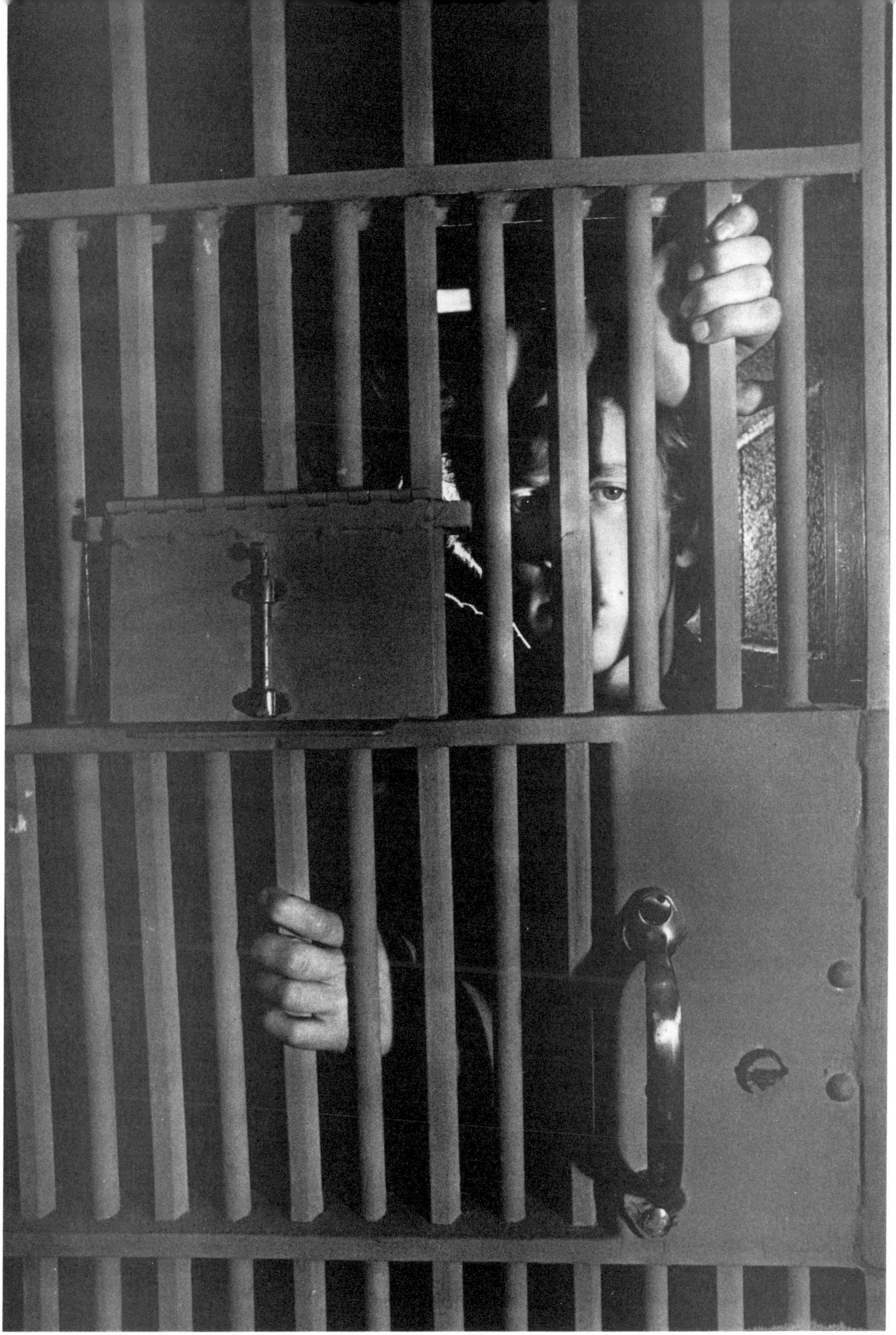

They looked so sure of themselves.

Just then the boy in front of him turned around.

"Hey, man, I've taken this ride before," said the stranger. "You're new, ain't ya? I can tell."

Danny stiffened. "I been on lots of rides," he said.

"Sure," the other boy replied. "But you're gonna wish you had a friend when you get there." The boy winked.

Danny wondered what he meant. But he decided not to probe any further. After a long drive, the bus turned onto a gravel road and passed through a gate. Danny saw some red brick buildings surrounded by green grass and trees. It looked like a nice place except for the high chain-link fence.

The bus stopped and the door opened. A man stepped onto the bus. "OK, boys. You'll get off one by one. Go to your assigned room and take your tests and your physical."

Danny spent two days alone before he talked to a counselor. He then received a cottage assignment, class schedule, work detail, and a list of rules. The counselor explained that if Danny followed the rules he would get "privileges." These included going to a movie once a month and receiving visitors. However, if he did not behave, he would be on lock-up. That meant little or no contact with the other boys. It also meant no sports and no visits from his family.

The next day, Danny awoke at 6 A.M. to the sound of a bell. He and the other boys in the large room bathed and dressed in communal shower rooms. None of the showers had curtains. The toilets were in one large room and had no partitions or doors. Danny hated the lack of privacy. He missed his home and family.

After breakfast Danny went to his first class, in arithmetic. He found that he already knew what was being taught. He wondered whether he would be able to switch to a more advanced arithmetic class.

In the afternoon, Danny was assigned to a trade shop to learn carpentry. He liked working with his hands. Soon he was absorbed in shaping and fitting two jointed pieces of wood. But then several boys began to argue about the use of a drilling machine. Others took sides, and a fight started. The instructor and several guards came to break up the fight. The two boys who started the fight were put in solitary cells for several days.

Danny asked for an appointment to see the counselor again. He did not want to get into any trouble while he was at the camp. He looked forward to the time when he could be free again. But the three months would be tough if he was bored in class. Also, it would be hard for him to stay out of trouble if other boys started a fight with him. He hoped the counselor would be able to help solve these problems.

Your Turn

What kind of a person is Danny? Do you think he will be helped or hurt by the camp?

2.
The day they closed the reform schools

The scene was the Shirley Industrial School, a reform school in Massachusetts for delinquent boys under the age of 17. In Cottage Nine sledgehammers were given to a group of young inmates. They hit the bars, locks, and walls, and began breaking down the building. Although their goal was knocking the walls down, the inmates were not trying to escape. Rather, they were starting a unique test as the state of Massachusetts sought a better way to run its juvenile corrections system.

The test began after a committee studied reform schools in Massachusetts. The committee was shocked. Its report said that, when young people in state reform schools were released, they were not ready to cope with the outside world. "It is no wonder that so many graduate to become inmates of our adult prisons," the committee said.

As a result of the report, the state began to close its reform schools. In one case, youngsters were sent for a month from state training schools to a college campus.

On campus

Each of the delinquents was given $12 a week in spending money and assigned to a college student for one month. The students were paid a small salary to take responsibility for the delinquents.

There was a shoplifting incident at the campus bookstore. Eleven youngsters ran away. But college officials agreed that the delinquents had given them less trouble than a conference of adults who had been on campus at the same time.

The test showed that young offenders could leave reform schools and live on the outside with very few incidents. As a result, other experiments have been tried.

For example, a program called Homeward Bound offers a rugged two-month course in outdoor survival for delinquent boys. For youths who can remain in their homes, neighborhood schools and recreation programs are used. Because there are so many programs, a young person who fails in one can try another.

Youngsters who are dangerous are kept in small maximum-security units. Each unit holds 12 youngsters. But only about 110 boys in the whole state are in these special programs.

Results

The results of these new programs have varied. Some of the young people have benefited from the program. Some haven't. For example, there have been runaways from some programs. Sometimes these youngsters return on their own.

But even for those youngsters who adjust to the program, the success rate is not promising. Recidivism (repeating a crime or crimes) is still high among the young people in the maximum-security units. So far the percentage of graduates who stay out of trouble is no better than in the days of training schools. Nevertheless, it is clear that these youths receive more humane treatment than they received in the days of the training schools.

Your Turn

1. What is the main difference between the programs described in this section and the training camp in the previous section?

2. The Massachusetts reforms have not improved the success rate in working with delinquent young people. What factors might affect the way a young person behaves after release?

3. Do you think delinquents should be locked up or placed in

Homeward Bound offers a rugged outdoor survival course for delinquent youths.

the new programs? Give reasons.

You might ask some of the following questions if a corrections or probation officer visits you in class. You could also ask these questions on a field activity (see page 200):

1. What are the duties of your job? How much contact do you have with the people in the institution?

2. What kinds of young people are there? What ages? What crimes have they committed?

3. Do you feel your work helps give a delinquent a better chance of making good when he or she is released?

4. How many young people "make it" or "go straight" when they get out of an institution like yours?

5. Is it dangerous to work in this institution? Are you given special training in self-defense or are you armed?

Field Activity

It will take some careful planning, but you will find it worthwhile if you can arrange a field visit to a youth correctional home, group home, or halfway house. Check with your teacher first. He or she may be able to help you over some rough spots in arranging the visit.

Observations. What is the general condition of the facility? What security measures are in force? What is the condition of each of the following areas? Sleeping. Recreation. Eating.

Questions. You might ask a staff member some of the following questions: What types of youths live here? How many are living here at this time? What services are provided to residents here? What is the single most important problem or challenge you face here as a staff member?

As part of your visit, you may have the opportunity to talk with one or more of the residents. You might want to ask some of the following questions: What is your normal day like here? What do you think about the food, sleeping quarters, rules, school, visits from relatives, grievances, vocational training, counseling? When will you get out? How do you feel about the future?

Conclusion. Do you believe facilities such as this one can help juvenile offenders?

Chapter 18
The Death Penalty

Capital punishment — the death penalty — is almost always in the news today. Americans debate such questions as: Is the death penalty allowed under our Constitution? When, if ever, should it be used? How should juries decide when to use it? In this chapter, you will learn more about the death penalty and will have the chance to debate these issues.

Many points of view

The following statements describe some common attitudes toward the death penalty. On a separate sheet of paper, list the numbers one to seven. Then read each of the following statements and mark down next to each number whether you: (a) strongly agree; (b) agree; (c) disagree; (d) strongly disagree with it.

1. Killing people who commit murder keeps other people from doing the same thing.

2. A person who commits murder or other serious crimes should pay with his or her life.

3. "An eye for an eye and a tooth for a tooth" is simple justice.

4. Some people can't be allowed in society because they are too dangerous. These people should be executed.

5. Anyone who places value on

201

human life cannot approve capital punishment.

6. "Thou shalt not kill" means even criminals should not be executed.

7. When the government executes a human being, it is committing murder.

Keep the sheet with your responses to these statements. At the end of this chapter, you will have the chance to react to the same statements again. Thus you will see if your views have changed as a result of reading this chapter.

1.
The ultimate penalty

At 10:03 the executioner pulled the cherry-red lever that dropped a bag of cyanide pellets into the tank of acid. Caryl Chessman breathed deeply for 20 seconds, then he raised his eyes to the ceiling, and his mouth fell open. At 10:05 he coughed. A minute later his face broke out with sweat and saliva dribbled from his mouth. He fell forward, his body straining against the straps; he cried and his body heaved. At 10:12 he was pronounced dead by a prison medical officer.

— from "Chronicles of San Quentin" by Kenneth Lamott

Capital punishment is an old practice. *Capital* comes from the Latin word *capita*, meaning head. Originally a person sentenced to death was beheaded. In the U.S. today, the death penalty is carried out through shooting, hanging, electrocuting, gassing, or lethal injection.

Throughout history, the death penalty has been used for serious crimes such as murder or treason. It has also been used to punish crimes such as picking pockets or stealing a loaf of bread. In the early 19th century in England, for example, there were 270 crimes that could be punished by death. Even children were hanged in public for acts which today would be considered no more serious than shoplifting.

The death penalty has been used throughout history for serious crimes — and also for crimes that today are not considered serious. Above, a public beheading in 14th-century France. Below, a 19th-century American criminal is hanged. Previous page, hanging of some petty criminals in 16th-century England.

In the U.S., a large number of crimes were also punished by death. Gradually, however, public protest reduced the number of capital crimes. Today the death penalty is outlawed in Britain. In the U.S., each state has the power to set its own penalties for crimes. Some states do not allow capital punishment. Others impose it only for certain kinds of murders. A few treat acts such as kidnapping as capital crimes.

2.
The controversy

People have argued the rights and wrongs of capital punishment for many years now. The following sections summarize the arguments on each side. Which do you agree with?

For capital punishment

a. Capital punishment keeps some people from committing serious crimes. It is hard to say how well this "deterrent" works. But common sense says that people who fear being caught will hesitate to murder if they think they will be punished by death.

b. If a person takes another life, he should pay for the act by giving up his or her own life. "An eye for an eye and a tooth for a tooth." This is a just punishment.

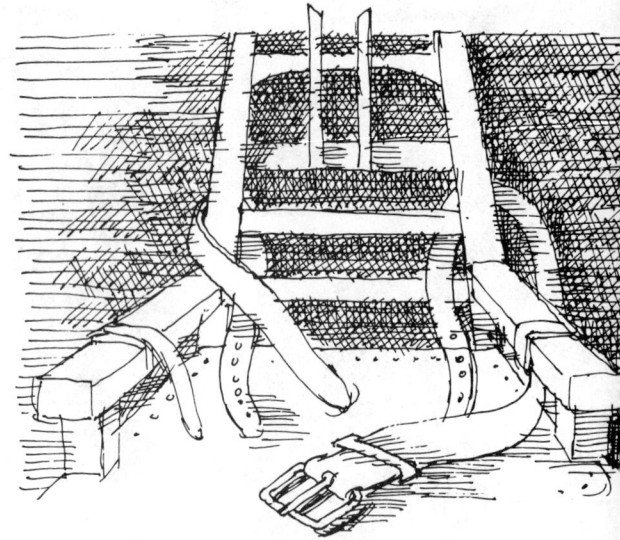

c. Capital punishment does not go against "due process of law." It is reserved for only the most serious crimes. It is not lightly handed out. Jurors are told to consider it very carefully. There are many steps in the appeals process before it is carried out.

Against capital punishment

a. Capital punishment does not stop people from committing murder. In states which have abolished the death penalty, murder rates have declined or remained the same. Most people who commit crimes do not believe they will be caught.

b. Capital punishment is a wrongdoing on top of a wrongdoing. It does not help the victim of the original crime. Locking a criminal up for the rest of his or her life is punishment enough.

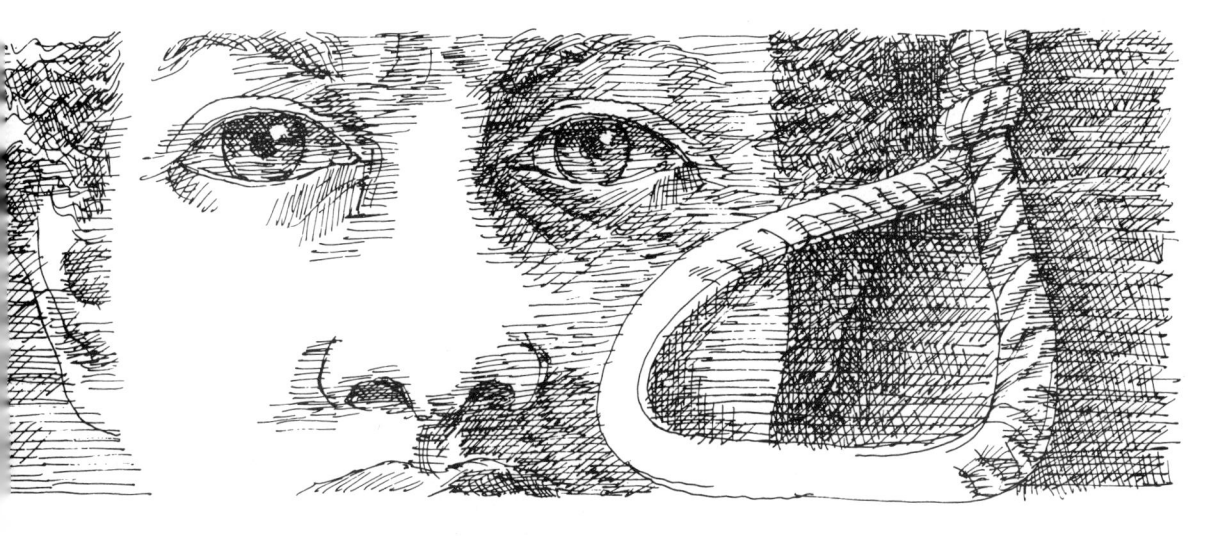

c. Capital punishment is not "due process." It is carried out mostly against those who are too poor to hire the best lawyers. Moreover, if an innocent person is convicted in error, there is no way of making amends.

Supreme Court rulings

During the 1970's the U.S. Supreme Court handed down a number of important rulings involving capital punishment. In a series of 1976 decisions, the Court declared that the death penalty was *not* a cruel and unusual punishment. That's because death is accepted by most Americans as the proper punishment for first-degree murder.

However, the justices also said that the *methods* for deciding when to impose the death penalty must be fair. They said that, before a jury can sentence a person to die, it must look at everything about the person and the crime, and make sure the defendant deserves death instead of life in prison. This means that a jury considering the death penalty has to be told to examine the defendant, his or her prior criminal record, and all the events that led to the crime.

This is not the final word on the death penalty. The issue is certain to come up in the Court over and over again. That's because the death penalty is one of the most controversial issues in our society. And it is the job of the Supreme Court to deal with those legal issues that divide Americans.

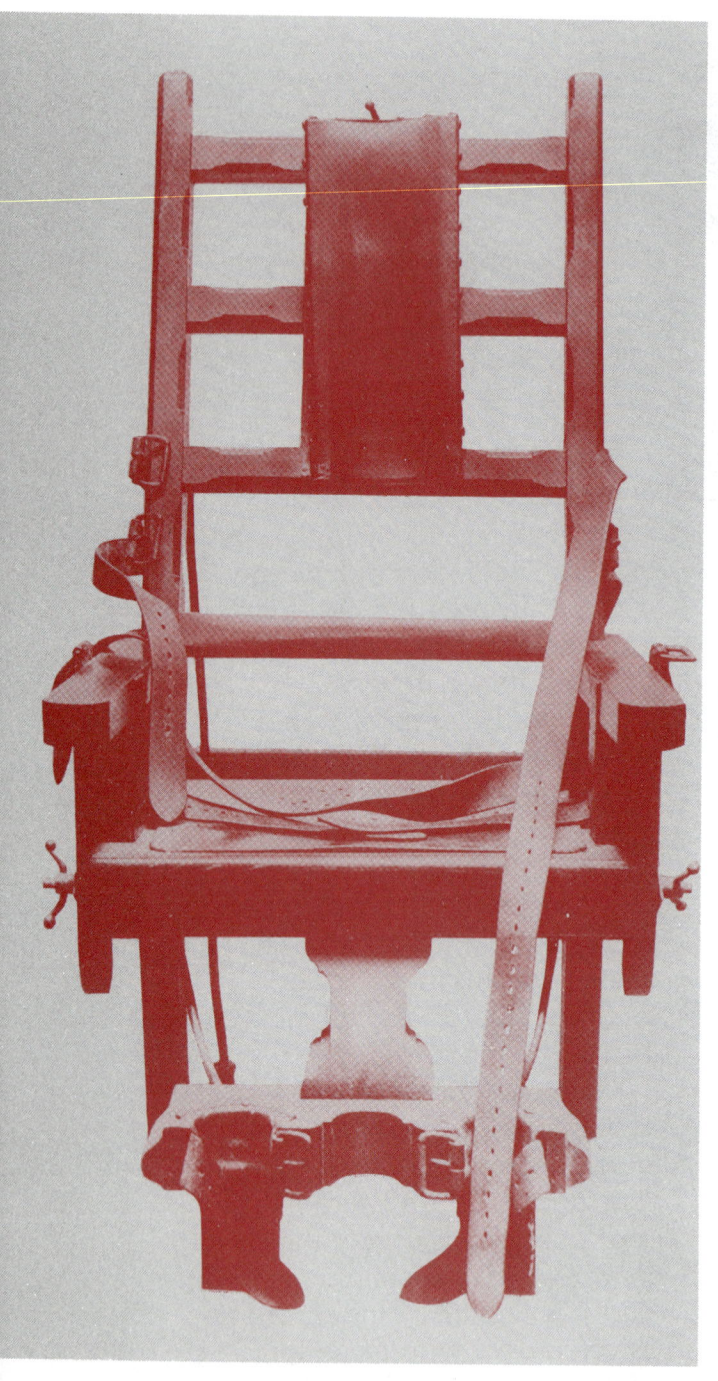

Your Turn

1. Surveys show that public support in America for capital punishment has increased over the last decade or so (49% in 1971; 65% in 1976; 66% in 1981). What might account for this increase in support for capital punishment?

2. One argument for the death penalty is the saying: "An eye for an eye and a tooth for a tooth." Do you agree with this saying? How do you feel about the arguments for and against capital punishment?

3. Some people feel that if capital punishment is to really prevent crime, all executions should be held in public. Do you agree with this position?

3.
A governor's dilemma

You are the governor of a state which allows capital punishment. However, state law allows the governor to grant a pardon to any person sentenced to prison. The governor can also change a death sentence to life imprisonment.

This is an election year, and recently your mail has been running 3–1 in favor of capital punishment. You have given much thought to this subject.

It is now 8:50 A.M. At 10 A.M., William Dow is scheduled to die in the electric chair for the crime of first-degree murder. His letter of appeal lies on your desk. You know the case well.

William Dow is 24 years of age. Although he had been in some minor trouble before, he had never been to prison. Now he has been convicted of murdering a friend, John Geddings. The killing happened during a drunken argument over a dice game. In an earlier argument, Geddings had struck Dow and broken his nose. Dow had left the scene of the game. A day later he returned with a gun he usually used for killing snakes. The argument resumed, and Dow shot Geddings. Dow claimed he had not meant to kill Geddings but had acted in self-defense. The jury did not accept Dow's claim and recommended that he be put to death.

In his appeal to you, Dow argues that capital punishment is immoral. Dow also says he is not a criminal but the victim of human misunderstanding. He regrets the killing of his friend deeply and says that he will never kill again. Dow says that the death penalty will not serve as a deterrent because it will not stop others who might kill in anger. Dow, therefore, pleads with you to spare him from the electric chair.

Consider the following questions in making your decision on Dow's plea:

a. As a state governor, what part of the Dow case seems most important to you? Why? Would you find this part of the case in most other murder cases?

b. What importance should you attach to public opinion about capital punishment? Would it make any difference if the mail had referred specifically to the Dow case?

c. What are your reactions to Dow's arguments in support of his plea? Would you decide to grant him a pardon or not? What would be your reasons for the decision?

Debriefing

Review the statements on the death penalty at the beginning of this chapter. Record your reactions to them on a separate sheet of paper. Don't look at the sheet you filled out before you started reading the chapter. Compare your reactions to these statements with those you recorded before reading the chapter. Have they changed? Remained the same? Why?

Compare the reactions of your classmates to these statements at the beginning and at the end of the chapter. Have they changed? If so, how? What reasons can you give for these changes? Have reactions remained the same? If so, why might this be the case?

Toward a Better System of Justice

During this part, you have had the chance to study the corrections system. You have read about the ideals — and the realities — of the system. Now it is time to sum up your views. Base these on your readings and any field activities, classroom visitors, and peer teaching you have been able to arrange. What parts of the system do you think work well? What parts don't? What changes do you think ought to be made?

Write a two-page essay summing up your ideas. What should be changed and what should be preserved in both the adult and the juvenile corrections systems?

The Bars: a Bibliography

America's Prisons; opposing viewpoints
edited by Bonnie Szumski, Greenhaven Press, 1985.
Contains information on prison life and views on prison conditions, excerpted from speeches, books, periodicals, and positions papers.

Doing Time: A Look at Crime and Prisons
by Phyllis E. Clark and Robin Lehrman, Hastings House, 1980.
Touches on the basic issues of crime and punishment. Also reviews major areas of concern in our prison system today.

The Roots of Crime
by Eda J. LeShan, Four Winds Press, 1981.
A number of ex-convicts get together to rehabilitate themselves. This book tells their stories. It deals not only with prison life but also with such broader issues as the causes of crime.

Violence! Our fastest-growing public health problem
by John Langone, Little, Brown & Co., 1985.
Discusses the causes and effects of various types of violent behavior, including prison riots, domestic violence, and assassination. Specific crimes such the New Bedford rape case of 1983 are examined in detail.

CONCLUSION

What Are the Choices?

Have you ever been the victim of a crime? Do you know someone who has?

Your answer to these questions must be yes. That's because everyone in the U.S. is a victim of crime. Crime costs all of us money through higher prices at stores. Crime means higher taxes to pay for anticrime measures. Thus, even if you haven't been mugged or had any of your possessions stolen, you are still one of crime's victims.

If we are to reduce crime, everyone must be a crime-fighter. In this section, you will read what some other students are doing to fight crime in their school. You will also get the chance to test how your values affect your views about fighting crime.

What can you do?

Violence seems to be sweeping our schools. Students and teachers have been beaten and killed. Damage to school property costs millions of dollars each year. Some schools have become places of danger, rather than places of learning.

What can be done to make schools safe?

"Having students as part of your security team is the only way I know to make schools safe," says Peter D. Blauvelt, Chief of Security for Prince Georges County, Maryland. Blauvelt was talking about a successful program in his county's schools. In it, junior and senior high school students took part in crime prevention programs in their schools.

The students formed security groups in each school. These groups made plans for dealing with vandalism, fighting, theft, and other crime problems. The groups were open to all students.

School officials worked with the security groups. The first task of the groups was to identify the most crucial security problems. Then the groups worked out actions to help make the school safer. Here are two examples of such activities:

• A "fight rumor box" has been installed in one school so students can alert school officials to possible violence.

• A patrol has been formed in another school to make hallways, locker areas, parking lots, and buildings more secure. No direct action is taken by the patrollers when they spot trouble. Their job is to report any problems to school officials.

Is it dangerous?

When the security groups were first formed, there was fear that some students might threaten or harm students in the groups. This did not happen. The students are not considered "snitches." That's because membership in the group is open to anyone.

School officials in the county are very pleased with the results of the program. For example, at one high school, there was a 98 percent decrease in vandalism and theft in the student parking lot during the first year of the program. The officials feel that the main reason for the program's success has been the fact that students have played a major role in solving the problems of crime in the school.

Note; This section is adapted from the *Bill of Rights Newsletter,* Spring 1977.

Your Turn

1. What was different about the anti-crime program described in this section? Why do you think it was successful?

2. To what extent should all citizens play an active part in preventing crime? What problems might be involved? Could they be overcome? Explain.

Cutting down on crime

How can the crime rate be reduced? The diagram below shows a variety of possibilities. Which do you think would help most in reducing crime? Are there any other ideas that you think would be effective? List the ideas in their order of importance, with the most important first.

What practical questions—such as cost—would be involved? Number the ideas in the order in which you think they would be easiest to carry out. Which ideas are both important and practical?

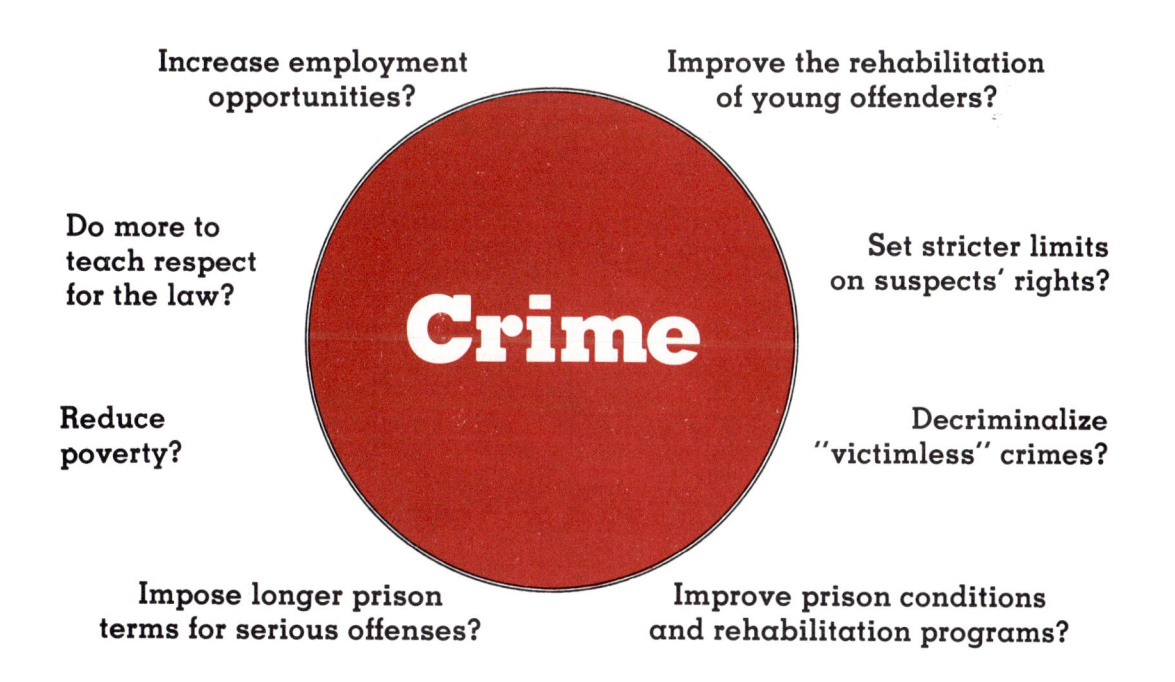

Increase employment opportunities?

Improve the rehabilitation of young offenders?

Do more to teach respect for the law?

Set stricter limits on suspects' rights?

Crime

Reduce poverty?

Decriminalize "victimless" crimes?

Impose longer prison terms for serious offenses?

Improve prison conditions and rehabilitation programs?

Glossary

Acquittal. In a criminal case, a finding that the defendant is not guilty.

Adversary system. A term for our system of justice in which the prosecuting attorney tries to establish the guilt of the defendant and the defense attorney tries to show errors in the prosecution's case.

Appellate court. Also called appeals court. A court which hears cases appealed to it from trial courts. It considers questions of law only. Questions of fact are considered in trial courts.

Arraignment. The procedure in which a person is brought to court and officially told of the charges against him or her. If the person pleads guilty, he or she is sentenced by the judge. If he or she pleads not guilty, the case is set for trial. Bail, if any, is also set at this time. (See also *Bail*.)

Arrest. Taking a person into custody on the basis of (1) an arrest warrant or (2) "probable cause" to believe that the person has committed a crime. (See also *Probable cause*.)

Bail. A sum of money set by a judge which is paid to the court on behalf of a person accused of a crime. Bail is supposed to assure that the person will return for trial. If the person fails to return, the bail money is kept by the court. If the person does return, bail is returned to him or her.

Bill of Rights. The first ten amendments to the Constitution of the U.S., which describe the rights and protections guaranteed to each citizen.

Booking. The formal listing by the police of the name of a person and the crime of which he or she is accused. This takes place after an arrest.

Capital punishment. The death penalty.

Case law. Laws made by the courts. For example, when a case is tried before the Supreme Court, the decision becomes a kind of law in that other similar cases will be viewed in a similar manner by lower courts. Such decisions are also called precedents. (See also *Precedents*.)

Challenge for cause. A lawyer's request to the judge that a person not be selected as a juror because he or she shows bias. (See also *Peremptory challenge*.)

Civil law. Laws which govern private transactions among individuals or businesses and which involve noncriminal matters. Civil laws describe what people can do if they feel they have been wronged by another person, or business, or by the government.

Civil suit. A court action brought by an individual who feels that he or she has been deprived of rights or has received some personal injury for which he or she should receive some compensation. A corporation or other business, as well as a government body, may also sue under civil law.

Common law. The term common law refers to all of the customs, legal traditions, and court decisions formed in England and later in America over several centuries. The common law provides the basis for the system of law used in the U.S.

Constitution. The basic principles which establish the structure and operation of government in the U.S. Both federal and state governments have written constitutions. The federal Constitution is the highest law of the land.

Constitutional law. The branch of law that is concerned with the meaning and interpretation of the rules and rights defined in the U.S. Constitution.

Consumer fraud. A type of crime which involves the cheating of consumers through trickery or misrepresentation—for example, when a merchant sells a used TV as brand-new. (See also *White collar crime*.)

Contempt of court. An act involving disrespect to the judge, or failure to obey the rules set by the judge.

Crime. In general, a crime is an act or an omission (failure to act) which is forbidden by law and for which the law imposes some punishment.

Criminal law. Laws which describe crimes and the penalties for committing crimes. (See also *Crime*.)

Cross-examination. In a trial, the questioning of a witness by a lawyer for the opposing side.

Custody. The physical confinement of a person after his or her arrest.

Delinquent. A juvenile who is judged by the court to be in need of treatment by the corrections system. (See also *Juvenile crime*.)

Deterrence. The idea that punishment of criminals will prevent, or deter, other crimes. For example, a person who considers stealing might be deterred by knowing that he or she will suffer a severe penalty if caught.

Discretion. The judgment of a law enforcement officer.

District attorney. The officer who represents the state in prosecuting criminal cases in court. In some states, he or she is called a *prosecuting attorney*.

Double jeopardy. Trying a person again for a crime of which he or she has already been found not guilty. This is a violation of our Constitution.

Due process. The idea that every person accused of a crime is entitled to a fair trial. This means that both fair laws and fair procedures must be used to judge the person. (See also *Bill of Rights*, *Constitution*, and various amendments.)

Eighth Amendment. The Eighth Amendment to the Constitution states that: "Excessive bail shall not be required, nor excessive fines imposed, nor cruel and unusual punishment inflicted." This amendment guarantees that fines or sentences given a person convicted of a crime will be fair, just, and humane. One of the major issues in the argument over capital punishment is whether it is "cruel and unusual punishment."

Equal protection. The idea that a law should apply in the same way to all persons affected by it and should not deprive any person of his or her constitutional rights.

Exclusionary rule. A rule set by the Supreme Court which holds that evidence obtained in violation of an individual's constitutional rights cannot be used in court against the person whose rights have been violated. (See also *Fourth Amendment* and *Probable cause*.)

Felony. A serious crime which is punishable by more than one year in a jail or prison.

Fence. A slang term for someone who receives stolen goods, pays for them, and then re-sells them at a profit.

Fifth Amendment. The Fifth Amendment to the Constitution protects a person against "self-incrimination." This means that no person has to answer questions about a crime of which he or she is accused or about his or her alleged part in it either to the police or to a court.

First Amendment. This Constitutional Amendment forbids the government to interfere with a citizen's freedom of speech, religious beliefs, freedom of the press, right to assemble in a peaceful manner, and right to petition

215

the government.

Fixed sentence. A prison sentence for a specific length of time. (See also *Indeterminate sentence*.)

Fourteenth Amendment. This Amendment to the Constitution gave citizenship to former slaves. The U.S. courts have said that the Amendment extends many of the protections in the Bill of Rights to citizens involved with the criminal justice systems in the 50 states. Originally the Bill of Rights was interpreted as applying only to the federal government.

Fourth Amendment. This Constitutional Amendment protects citizens against "unreasonable searches and seizures." It holds that searchers must first get a warrant from a judge before searching any private premises. For a search and/or seizure to be "reasonable," there must be evidence that a crime has been committed, and a strong likelihood that the person or place to be searched will yield the "fruits of the crime" or the person who has committed the crime. (See also *Probable cause*, *Search warrant*, and *Warrantless search*.)

Gag order. An order made by a judge which forbids publicity about a case. Usually, it forbids anyone involved in the case to speak about the case outside the courtroom.

Grand jury. A body of citizens who are sworn to inquire into crimes and other public offenses and to make indictments. Unlike a trial by jury, the hearings of the grand jury are secret. (See also *Indictments*.)

Grand theft, auto. A felony which involves the taking of an auto from its owner without the owner's permission and with the intention of keeping the auto permanently. (See also *Joyriding*.)

Habeas corpus. A Latin phrase meaning "you have the body." It is the requirement that a person in custody be brought before a judge "without delay," be informed of the charges against him and be freed on bail whenever the circumstances justify. A person in custody may demand to be brought before a judge using a document called a "writ of habeas corpus."

Halfway house. A temporary home for people released from penal institutions. The idea behind it is that certain people need a period to readjust to life "in the real world" when they leave prison. Persons living in halfway houses take part in the community through work, school, and other activities but live in the home with counselors and other prisoners going through the same period of adjustment.

Homicide. The unlawful killing of one human being by another.

Hot pursuit. A situation in which police officers chase a suspect or an escaped prisoner on foot or in an auto or other vehicle. No search or arrest warrant is needed in such a situation. (See also *Arrest* and *Warrantless search*.)

Hung jury. A jury which is unable to reach a unanimous decision or, if unanimity is not required, a majority decision. In such an instance, the case may be re-tried before another jury. (See also *Double jeopardy* and *Due process*.)

Indeterminate sentence. A prison sentence for an indefinite period of time, say "one year to life." Under this system of sentencing, a prisoner is released if and when the parole board decides he or she has been rehabilitated. (See also *Rehabilitation*.)

Indictment. A written accusation prepared by a grand jury charging that a certain person has committed a crime. (See also *Grand jury* and *Information*.)

Information. A written accusation made against an accused person directly by the district attorney's office without an investigation by a grand jury. (See also *Grand jury*, *Indictment*, and *District attorney*.)

Joyriding. Taking a car for a drive

without the owner's permission, but with the intention of returning it. (See also *Grand theft, auto*.)

Judicial review. The power of the U.S. Supreme Court to examine federal and state laws and actions and to decide whether these laws and actions are constitutional. (See also *Constitution, Constitutional law, Case law,* and *Precedent*.)

Juvenile crime. Crimes committed by persons under a certain age set by each of the states. Usually that age is 18.

Miranda rights. Rights possessed by persons who are arrested by police. As a result of *Miranda v. Arizona*, 1966, the Supreme Court ruled that before being questioned by police, an arrested person must be told of his or her rights. These are: to have the help of an attorney, to have an attorney supplied by the state if he or she can't afford one, to remain silent, to stop the questioning any time he or she chooses, and to know that anything he or she does may be used later in court.

Misdemeanor. A crime, but one that is less serious than a felony. It is punishable by a fine and/or imprisonment in county jails, but not in state prison. (See also *Felony*.)

Organized crime. Crime conducted by a group of persons organized for that purpose. Organized crime often involves such crimes as gambling, loansharking, and narcotics sale.

Own recognizance. A program for releasing some persons accused of a crime before their trial. If a judge agrees, a person can be released without bail. (See also *Arraignment* and *Bail*.)

Pardon. To forgive all or part of a prisoner's sentence. A *full* pardon, in addition, restores to a convicted person all rights and the vote, which he or she may have lost as a result of the conviction. (See also *Parole*.)

Parole. The release of an offender from a correctional institution before he or she completes sentence. (See also *Pardon*.)

Parole board. A board appointed by the governor of a state whose main duty is to grant pardons and/or set terms of sentences of prisoners. The board also can revoke pardons.

Peremptory challenge. A lawyer's refusal to select a juror without giving any reason. The prosecuting and defense attorneys in a trial may each use a fixed number of peremptory challenges. (See also *Challenge for cause*.)

Perjury. Lying under oath — for example, when a witness at a trial does not tell the truth. Perjury is a criminal offense.

Plaintiff. The person who starts a civil lawsuit by accusing another of committing a civil wrong.

Plea bargain. The process by which prosecuting and defense attorneys, with the permission of the defendant, agree that the defendant will plead guilty to a lesser charge. One purpose of plea bargaining is to reduce the load of cases on the court system.

Precedents. Decisions made by federal and state supreme courts. Precedents are important because they may be used in later cases to show that certain actions are legal or illegal. (See also *Case law*.)

Preliminary hearing. A court procedure during which a judge decides whether or not there is enough evidence to bring an accused person to trial.

Premeditation. The planning of a crime for some time before it was committed. Premeditation is one of the key aspects of first-degree murder.

Probable cause. A strong belief, based on facts, that a crime has been committed, that a certain person has committed a crime, and/or that evidence relating to the crime exists. For example, in issuing a search warrant, a judge must have probable cause. That is, evidence must be brought before him or her showing that there is a reason for conducting a search. (See also *Search warrant* and *Arrest*.)

Probation. A type of sentence which requires a person convicted of a crime to follow certain rules or conditions, often under the supervision of a probation officer. Probation is usually considered an alternative to prison.

Public defender. A lawyer employed by the government to represent defendants who do not have or cannot afford to employ their own lawyers.

Reasonable force. The amount of force, and no more, a police officer needs to make an arrest and prevent the escape of a person who is being arrested. (See also *Arrest*.)

Recidivism. The committing of further crimes by offenders with previous convictions.

Rehabilitation. Helping a convicted person change his or her behavior so that he or she can lead a useful and productive life in society.

Search warrant. A legal document issued by a judge describing the location to be searched by law enforcement officers and the item(s) and/or person(s) to be seized. For example, a search warrant for a stolen television may not include the possibility of looking in the desk drawer or medicine cabinet where the television could not fit, but may include looking in the living room, bathtub, basement, attic, or other places where the set could be concealed. (See also *Fourth Amendment*, *Warrantless search*, and *Probable cause*.)

Sentence. A punishment for a crime.

Sixth Amendment. This Amendment assures every citizen, from the time he or she is arrested, the right to a "speedy" and fair trial and the right to the help of a lawyer.

Status offense. A non-criminal act by a juvenile. The juvenile may be taken into custody and/or found delinquent by the Juvenile Court. The same act, if committed by an adult, would not be cause for arrest. (See also *Delinquent* and *Juvenile crime*.)

Statute of limitations. The requirement that a person be indicted for a crime within a certain length of time. After that time the person who may have committed the crime cannot be prosecuted for it. The length of time varies with the crime and the state.

Street crime. A class of crimes usually involving force or violence, such as murder, assault, robbery, and rape.

Subpoena. A court order requiring a person to appear in court to give testimony.

Verdict. The decision made as to the facts of a case by a judge or jury.

Victimless crimes. Crimes which have no direct victims other than the person who commits the crime — for example, drunkenness, drug offenses, gambling. These crimes may also involve acts that are considered social problems. The courts have heavy case loads of victimless crimes. Efforts have been made to "decriminalize" these acts and find other ways to deal with them.

Warrantless search. A search conducted by police officers without a warrant. Such action is legal under certain conditions in which it would be impossible to obtain a search warrant. (See also *Fourth Amendment* and *Probable cause*.)

Wiretapping. The use of electronic "bugging" devices to listen to and record people's telephone conversations without their knowledge. (See also *Fourth Amendment* and *Exclusionary rule*.)

White collar crime. A class of crimes which are usually job-related. Among them are embezzlement (taking money entrusted to one's care), bribery, price-fixing, and consumer fraud. White collar crimes often involve some form of theft which takes place without the use of force. (See also *Consumer fraud*.)

Index

Adversary system, 114
Appeals, 147
Arizona, 89
Arrest, 63, 76, 78, 80; and constitutional rights, 82–95; role play, 85
Attica State Prison, 174–175

Bail, 21, 22, 115–117
Bailbondsperson, 115
Bibliography, 59, 109, 159, 209
Bill of Rights, 52–58, 71
Bill of Rights Newsletter, 168, 176, 187
"Bobbies," 64
Booking, 19, 84
Boston, establishment of police force, 64
"Burden of proof," 137

California, 166
Capital punishment, *see* Death penalty
Chessman, Caryl, 202
Chicago, 88
Cigarette box search, *see Gustafson v. Florida*
Civil law, 50–51
Civil rights, 52
Confessions, 86–91, 93–95
Consent in warrantless search, 74
Constitution, U.S., 52–59, 75, 147, 201; *see also* various Amendments
Crime and "permissiveness," 41–42; and poverty, 41; and unemployment, 42; and youth, 41; causes of, 41–43; history of, in U.S., 38; organized, 36; victims of, 38, 211
Criminal law, 50–51, 52–58
Criminals, characteristics of, 35–36, 38

Dallas, 93
Death penalty, 45, 201–208
Defense lawyer, 124–125, 139, 142
Delinquency, 157, 182–184
Denver, 93
District attorney, 81, 122–124, 128, 134, 135, 139, 140

Double jeopardy, 58
Due process, 58, 114–115

Eighth Amendment, 58, 201–202
Emergency, in warrantless search, 75
Equal protection of the law, 115
Escobedo v. Illinois, 88–89, 91, 147
Ethics, 126–127
Evidence in a criminal trial, 80–81, 131–133
"Exclusionary rule," 80–81
Ex post facto, 57–58

Federal Bureau of Investigation (FBI), 64
Felony, 25, 84
Felony-murder law, 139
Field activities, 44, 69, 119, 127, 200
Fifth Amendment, 58
"Firearms policies," 99
Fixed sentences, 190–191
Florida, 76, 77
Fourth Amendment, 58, 71–73, 74, 77, 80

Gault, In Re, 151–152
Glossary, 214–218
Grand jury, 58, 112, 114
Grand theft, auto, 22, 25
Gustafson v. Florida, 75–80

Habeas corpus, 57
Hearsay, 131
Hot pursuit, 74

Indeterminate sentencing, 185–187
Issues of fact and law, 136, 147

Joyriding, 21, 25
Judge, role of, 128, 139, 145–146
Jury duty, 8
Jury system, 112, 130–131, 147
Juvenile corrections, 194–200
Juvenile court hearing, 25–28, 149–150
Juvenile intake, 25–26
Juvenile justice, 11, 99, 148–159
Juveniles, rights of, 99–100, 151–152

219

...w, 47–51; and daily life, 50–51; need for laws, 49–50
Law and order, 63, 71
Lawyers and ethics, 126–127; and law, 120–127
Los Angeles, 46

Marshall, Thurgood, 78–79
Maryland, 212
"Massachusetts experiment," 197–198
Memphis Five, 11–33
Miranda rights, 16, 19, 90–91
Miranda v. Arizona, 89–91, 147
Misdemeanor, 25, 84
Murder, 39, 45
"Mutt and Jeff" approach, 86

New York, City, 38, 64, 96; State, 174
Nightwatch, 63

Opinion poll, 44

Parole, 185–193
Parole boards, 185, 187–189
Peel, Sir Robert, 63–64
Peer teaching, 46, 99, 103, 193, 207
Penal Code, 136
Pennsylvania System, 163–164
Petit jury, 112
Phoenix, 89
Plain view, in warrantless search, 75
Plea bargaining, 23, 25, 117–118
Police and privacy, 70–81; arrest, 82–95; history of, in U.S., 63–64; interrogation, 86–91; killed in line of duty, 98; local control, 64–65; power, 96–109; rights of, 100
Police test, role play, 103–107
Police work, danger of, 98–99
Preliminary hearing, 22
Pretrial release, 116–117
Prison, 31–33, 151, 161, 168–169; history of, in U.S., 163–165; life in, 174–177; reform, 167
Prisoners' rights, 177–178
Privacy, 71–73
Probable cause, 71, 74, 77, 84
Probation, 150–151, 168, 179–184
Prosecution, *see* District attorney

Public defender, 22, 115, 117, 124–125, 156, 157
Punishment, cruel and unusual, 58

Quakers, 163–164
Questioning, police, 86–91

Reasonable doubt, 137
Recidivism, 166, 198
Rehabilitation of criminals, 165
Rehnquist, William, 78
Resource person, 81, 85, 107, 115, 117, 125, 136, 139, 155, 162, 179, 182, 185, 187, 194
Right to counsel, 88–90
Rights of accused, 56–58
Runaways, 153–154

San Francisco, 38
Search and seizure, *see* Fourth Amendment
Search during an arrest, 75
Search warrants, *see* Warrants, search
Sentencing, 31, 190; role play, 168–173
Seventh Step, 191, 193
Shirley Industrial School, 197
Shoplifting, 43–44, 68–69, 154–155
Sixth Amendment, 58, 84, 88–90
Squeal room, 86
State police, 64
Stop-and-frisk, 75, 100
Supreme Court, U.S., 56, 75, 77, 78, 80, 86, 88, 90, 91, 114, 124, 147, 152, 178, 205

Training camp, juvenile, 194–197
Trial by combat, 112
Trial by ordeal, 112
Trials, criminal: appeals, 147; history of, 112–114; mock, 138–147; procedure, 128–137; right to a speedy and fair, 58, 111–119, 147; role of witnesses, 133–135

Victimless crimes, 43

Warrantless searches, 74–75, 75–80
Warrants, search, 58, 72, 73, 80, 102
Watergate, 126
Witnesses at a trial, 128, 139, 140–141, 144–145
Writs of assistance, 71

PHOTO CREDITS: Page ii, 10, Fred Burell • 12–33, Richard Hutchings, • 37, UPI • 40, Magnum/Seitz • 42, Monkmeyer/Cron • 45 (top), Culver; (bottom), Bettmann Archive • 48 (top), Historical Society of Pennsylvania; (bottom), British Museum • 50, Library of Congress • 53–55, Richard Hutchings • 57, Library of Congress • 60, Fred Burell • 63, Alfred J. Young Collection, New York • 64, 65 (left), New York City Police Museum; (right), Monkmeyer/Conklin • 66, Dan Nelken • 68, Jay Dorin • 74, Photo Researchers/Lettau • 81, Stock, Boston/Franken • 85, Dan Nelken • 86, "Under Arrest: Operation Street Encounter."/Gene Lesser and Associates • 89, Wide World • 92, Magnum/Adelman • 94, Magnum/Harbutt • 98, Wide World • 100, Magnum/Freed • 101, UPI • 104 (top and middle), Magnum/Webb; (bottom) Stock, Boston/Schuyler • 110, Fred Burell • 113 (top), Henry E. Huntington Library; (bottom left), *The Masters of the Bench of the Inner Temple,* photo courtesy A. C. Cooper, London; (bottom right) Bettmann Archive • 114, Black Star/Michelle Bogre • 116, Magnum/C. Capa • 118, Stock, Boston/Herwig • 125, Scholastic Inc./Jeremiah Bean • 149, Monkmeyer/Conklin • 150, Magnum/Harbutt • 152, Magnum/Glinn • 154 (top), Wide World; (bottom), Magnum/Seitz • 160, Fred Burell • 162, Free Library of Philadelphia • 163 (top), U.S. Department of Justice • 164, Library of Congress • 165, Monkmeyer/Conklin • 167, Monkmeyer/Strickler • 169, Magnum/Harbutt • 177, Black Star/Kretz • 181, Magnum/Burri • 183 (top), Magnum/Berry; (bottom), Monkmeyer/Rogers • 191, Jay Dorin • 192, Stock, Boston/Wolinsky • 195, Dan Nelken • 197, Magnum/Glinn • 199, Stock, Boston/Berrdt • 200, Magnum/Harbutt • 202, British Museum • 203 (top), Mansell Collection • 206, Bettmann Archive.